Nicolette House

Summary: Maddie struggles to perform in a figure skating competition when she keeps her problems bottled up inside.

ISBN: 978-0-9819342-2-8

Library of Congress Control Number: 2010924116

Printed in the United States of America

Sporting Chance Press™, Inc.
1074 Butler Drive
Crystal Lake, IL 60014
Visit us at www.sportingchancepress.com

Manufactured by Thomson-Shore, Dexter, MI (USA); 566TB563, April, 2010

To my mom and dad and all those
who helped me succeed in the sport.

1

Lesson at Dawn

BRRR! When her alarm went off at 5:45 on the second Saturday of October, Madison Albright's eyes flew open. Most girls would groan about waking up this early, but not Madison. She jumped out of bed, lifted her arms high above her head, and stretched.

She walked to her wardrobe and pulled out her favorite pink velvet skating outfit. Holding the dress in front of her, Madison looked in the mirror and sighed. The dress made her eyes shine. It was also her lucky practice dress and she would put it to good use getting ready for the regional figure skating championships scheduled for the following week.

"You ready?" called Madison's mom.

"Be down in a minute!" Madison smiled to herself. Mom was always up on time, ready to drive her to practice.

She heard her mom's signal: two beeps. Madison knew she was running late and flew down the stairs, grabbing a hoodie to wear in the cool autumn dawn.

"Feeling ready for regionals?" her mother asked as Madison slid into the car.

Madison grew quiet, hesitating. She didn't want to tell her mom how nervous she was about the competition.

"Of course I am. Liz says 'Everything is going great!' I couldn't be more excited," Madison replied, reporting her coach's opinion but hiding her own. But she was certain that Liz, her main coach, was preparing her for the regional event.

Madison knew just what to say to calm her mother's nerves. If only Madison could do that for herself!

1

"Well, I'm glad to hear it. You work so hard, sweetheart. Liz said that you have a good chance of placing high—maybe even winning if you skate well."

"If?"

"I meant *when,* Madison. Don't be so touchy. You feel ready, right?"

"Right…right, I am."

Mother and daughter rode quietly until Mrs. Albright pulled up outside the Arctic Circle Ice Arena. Madison reached over and gave her a hug.

"Bye, Mom. Thanks for the ride."

Madison jumped out of the car, taking deep breaths. *It's not about where you place,* she reminded herself, *but how well you skate.* Wasn't that what Liz always told her? *But then, why did she tell Mom that I could win?* Madison wondered.

The ice was already crowded when she stepped on to warm up. The biggest competition of the year brought the rink's skaters in for added icetimes this week. The Upper Great Lakes Region included seven states with more than six hundred skaters participating in the regional competition. Madison was skating in the Intermediate Ladies events, a level in which a hundred forty five skaters would compete.

During warm-up, Madison imagined the upcoming competition. If she won or placed in the top four, she could go on to compete at U.S. Figure Skating's Junior National Championships. If not, she could not qualify again until the next year. She warmed up her crossovers and spins, then her jumps. A huge smile spread across her face as she felt the speed and power with which she skated. She loved the sport and the exhilaration of skating more than anything.

"Madison," Liz called her over to the boards. "Run through your competition warm-up and then we'll run through your long program."

Madison took a deep breath, then skated to the blue line to begin her warm-up routine. She felt the familiar butterflies in her stomach as she warmed up the first element of the two-and-a-half-minute long program—a layback spin. As the competition grew close, Madison knew the time to learn new skills was over. Now it was all about drilling what she knew. Madison continued warming up her jumps—a double Salchow, double flip-double toe, and a double Lutz. She was just finishing her footwork when Liz called, "Time. Okay, go get in your starting position. Let's run your long program now."

Madison grinned. She loved her long program, set to flamenco music that matched the style of her hot pink and black competition dress.

"Oh, and do the double axel this time," Liz reminded her.

Great, just as I was calming down, Madison grumbled. She hadn't warmed that jump up on purpose. The double axel was the only jump in the whole program that worried Madison. At least as her first program element, she could get it out of the way soon.

The first strums of the Spanish guitar jerked Madison away from her thoughts and she quickly centered herself to concentrate on her program. She started out edging, gathering speed before she entered her double axel.

Breathe in, breathe out, bring your leg through, Madison repeated to herself. In the blink of an eye, the jump was over and Madison moved on to the next element. She breathed a sigh of relief and relaxed throughout the rest of her routine. As she finished her combination spin, she heard applause in the stands. She looked up and saw a tall woman with short black hair applauding her. *Who's that?* she thought to herself.

"Skate laps," Liz coached.

Madison skated two laps to catch her breath and stopped in front of Liz.

"That was pretty good. You need to skate just like that on Sunday. I noticed that you were really tense at the beginning, but after you landed the double axel you were fine."

"That jump just makes me nervous, I guess."

"Why? You do it all the time."

Madison shrugged.

"See?" challenged Liz. "You can't answer. There is nothing to worry about. You've worked hard. You just have to skate Sunday like you do in practice. What happens after that is out of your hands."

Madison nodded.

"Okay," Liz continued, "let's run the long program in sections and then you're done. Tomorrow we'll run your short."

The rest of the practice ran smoothly, and Madison packed away her skates feeling confident. After her cool-down and stretching, Madison went outside to look for her mother's car. Just then, the woman who had applauded her stepped up.

"Hi. I'm Rebecca Boyle," she said, shaking Madison's hand. "Are you competing at regionals next weekend?"

"Yeah, I am. Intermediate Ladies."

"That's great. I'm working the competition in Minnesota, so maybe I'll see you. I watched your program today. It was wonderful."

"Thanks. It's my favorite piece so far."

"Well, skate like that and you'll probably win. We'll keep an eye out for you." Rebecca winked at Madison just as Madison's mom pulled up. Madison stood frozen in thought for a moment and then jumped into the car.

"Hi, honey. Who was that woman? You look unsettled."

"That was Rebecca Boyle. She's volunteering at regionals. She likes the way I skate and she says if I skate like I did today I could win."

"Isn't that great to hear before you compete?"

Madison was quiet. Her mom went on, "So practice went well? I said your hard work would pay off. Feeling better?"

"Oh, yeah. Yeah. I feel great."

Not really, Madison thought to herself. She not only had her coach and her mothers' high expectations to meet, but now strangers like Rebecca Boyle had thoughts about what she could accomplish. Madison's own personal expectations were very high, but she didn't want other people to get into her head. And now they had done it! As soon as she got home, Madison raced to her bedroom and buried her face in her pillow to block everything out.

2

A Surprising Prize

Madison awoke from her usual Saturday morning nap. *I wish I could've slept over at Jordan's house last night,* she thought gloomily as she stared out her window. It had been raining since yesterday and her mood matched the gray sky perfectly. Madison realized she couldn't have gone out this weekend no matter what. She needed to rest up for her competition. She no longer hung out with friends on weekends before big events. It was one of the sacrifices required of a competitive figure skater.

Sometimes Madison didn't mind staying home because she used the time to catch up on her homework. This weekend she did more than that. She used homework to focus energy on anything but skating. By two o'clock, Madison was three assignments ahead in math and two ahead in English. She'd even finished her history paper and an extra credit assignment. After packing up her schoolwork, Madison kept busy watching movies, reading, looking through magazines—anything to fill her thoughts.

"This weekend isn't what I need! I'm not rested; I'm going crazy!" she said in exasperation.

"What was that, honey?" Madison's dad poked his head in the doorway.

"Was I talking out loud?" asked Madison meekly.

"Yes, but I couldn't quite make everything out. What's up?"

"It's not important. Don't worry, Dad. I was, uh, just trying to memorize a speech for school." Madison knew it was wrong to lie, but she didn't want to worry him.

"Okay. Dinner in fifteen," her dad said, closing her door. A few minutes later flavorful aromas wafted toward Madison's door. Suddenly she was incredibly hungry. After waiting fifteen minutes, Madison bounded down the stairs two at a time.

"Mmm, mmm. What are you cooking?" Madison asked.

"Salmon with mashed potatoes. Your favorite." Madison's mom winked and tapped Madison on the nose. Just as she was about to thank her mom for making this special dinner, they heard loud bass thumps blaring from just outside the house.

"Dylan!" Madison's dad groaned.

Dylan, Madison's older brother, had just turned sixteen and was taking full advantage of his new driving privileges. A few seconds later, he appeared in the doorway.

"Dylan, how many times have I told you not to drive up blasting the music and damaging your eardrums along with everyone else's in the neighborhood!"

"Sorry! It's not like I don't pay attention. Three months and no tickets yet."

Dylan grinned. He hitched up his jeans, ran his fingers through his dark wavy hair, and turned to walk out of the kitchen.

"Dinner's ready," Mom called after him.

"Yeah, yeah," he muttered and stomped upstairs.

Dylan was brusque, but Madison still looked up to him. He was so cool and didn't care what anybody thought of him. He listened to music, did his own thing, and didn't worry about being perfect for anyone.

Madison heard Dylan start a shower and knew dinner would be postponed. She glanced quickly at her mother and saw her fervently banging pots and pans together, muttering angrily. Mom hated to have her dinner get cold. Dylan made tonight's shower extra long.

After nearly thirty minutes, everyone gathered at the dinner table. Dylan was the last to sit.

"So glad you could grace us with your presence," Mom said sarcastically, slapping mashed potatoes on Dylan's plate.

"Julie, please!" Madison's father pleaded. "How was work, son?"

"Good. You know. We sold a lot of CDs and a shipment comes in this weekend, so I have to work extra hours to restock shelves."

"Oh, my hardworking children," smiled Dad, "and Madison, how is skating coming? Regionals this week! You ready?"

"Yeah, it's no big deal, right? 'Skate like you do in practice.' Skate clean and all that. I'm ready. My jumps are consistent and I've been doing perfect run-throughs all week."

"Good. Glad to hear it." Her father took a deep breath. "My week was good, too. I did a lot of thinking. I was wondering: how do you guys feel about expanding the family?"

"What, like a baby?" Dylan lifted his eyes off his plate for the first time, alarm crossing his face.

Dad rolled his eyes. "No, Dylan. A different type of addition. One with fur and four legs."

Madison's eyes lit up. She knew where her dad was going with this. "A puppy! Really?"

Dad nodded. She had wanted a puppy for almost a year, but her parents had kept telling her the time wasn't right.

"When are we getting her? What kind of dog will she be?"

"Hold on a sec. I didn't say we were getting a puppy right now. I just said it was something I was thinking about," explained Mr. Albright.

"Hey, Dad, why don't you buy the puppy if Madison wins her competition? Yeah, that way the puppy is her reward for a great skate," Dylan suggested.

Dad contemplated that, then slowly said, "Yes I think that's a great idea. Madison, if you win regionals, I'll buy you a puppy."

"And if I don't place first?"

"What kind of dog are you gonna get, Maddie?" Dylan asked before Dad could reply.

"Oh, I don't know. I really like Chihuahuas and golden retrievers, and pugs, and labs, teacup poodles...."

"We get it. You'd like one of each," Dylan laughed.

Madison daydreamed through the rest of dinner. She really wanted that puppy. If she just skated well enough....After the family had finished discussing activities of the upcoming week, Madison cleared her plate, stacked dishes by the sink, and headed straight for her room. That night she dreamed of Chihuahuas and poodles doing double axels.

chapter

3

School Days

Monday morning the sun woke Madison. She felt surprisingly rested. Only three days left before she and her mother drove to Minnesota for regionals.

Madison dressed and made herself breakfast. After stacking her dishes, Madison packed and dumped her backpack in Dylan's car. She checked her watch: 7:45. School started in fifteen minutes. She could not be late today! Her teachers were already upset she'd miss school for the competition. No need to give them another reason to be angry.

Madison threw the door to her brother's room wide open—no Dylan. She looked around, bewildered, until she saw a heap of blankets in his bed. Dylan wasn't even awake yet! She ripped the bedclothes away. Still he didn't budge. She grabbed a free pillow and swatted his head.

"Hey! Get up! We have to go!" Madison yelled at him.

"What? No, it's Sunday," Dylan said groggily.

"It's 7:50 on Monday morning! I'm gonna be late and so are you! You have to drop me off before you drive to high school."

"Oh, would you relax? So you're late one day. Big deal."

"It *is* a big deal. Everything needs to be perfect this week so I don't go to regionals stressed out!" Madison wailed.

"You? Never gonna happen," said Dylan getting up. He flung a pillow at Madison. "Now get out of here so I can get dressed."

Madison slammed the door.

Five minutes later Dylan came downstairs. Madison already sat in the car, arms crossed.

"You don't shower or eat or anything?" Madison snapped as Dylan slid into the driver's seat.

"Not on days I oversleep. Besides, I have gym first period. I'll shower after."

Dylan shifted to reverse and sped down the driveway. Madison rolled her eyes. Luckily, her school was only five minutes from home, so she walked into homeroom just as the bell rang. Madison breathed a sigh of relief. Now that she had arrived on time, she regretted yelling at Dylan. He had been thoughtful to volunteer to drive her to school once he got his license and she wasn't being very nice in return. He was doing her mom a big favor by letting her sleep in on nonskating mornings, and Madison knew her mother appreciated it. Madison vowed to try to appreciate it, too.

By lunchtime, the morning's confrontation was forgotten and Madison focused on her afternoon practice.

"Hey, Madison!" her friend Jordan Riley greeted, bouncing up to her. Jordan and Madison had been best friends since kindergarten. Just by the way Jordan was smiling, Madison knew that Jordan had good news to share.

"You'll never guess what happened!" Jordan exclaimed, her strawberry blond curls bouncing with excitement. "You know the Halloween fair on Friday night? Tyler asked me if I would go with him! Can you believe it? He's going to—okay, his mom is going to—pick me up and everything!" Jordan's cheeks were flushed bright red now as she tried to catch her breath.

Madison hugged her friend. "Oh, that's so great! It's like a real date. What will you wear?" Madison knew that going to the fair with Tyler was a big deal to Jordan. She'd had a major crush on Tyler since fourth grade. Now she was finally going to spend special time with him.

"I have, like, three outfits in my head already. And we're going for ice cream after, so I have to dress for that, too. My outfit should say flirty yet sophisticated, stylish yet classy, fun but not...."

As her friend talked, Madison's thoughts drifted back to regionals. She visualized the short program. She had just imagined landing her double Lutz combination flawlessly when Jordan said, "...and it's gonna be so much fun! You have to be there, too. We have to find you a date. Then we can all go together. Our first double date!"

Madison knew that Jordan took this whole invitation way too far, but that was Jordan. She got excited about everything and constantly looked for her life's next adventure.

"I have regionals this week, remember? I'll be in Minnesota on Friday."

Jordan's eyes widened. "Oh shoot. Sorry, I knew that. I shouldn't make such a big deal about all of this. You can't even go to the fair."

"No, no. I'm used to missing things. Have fun and I'll hear about it when I get back." Madison squeezed her hand. "Gotta run. Practice."

"Have fun. I'll call you. You have to help me pick out my outfit."

Madison grinned, "You bet," and turned toward her locker. She was happy for Jordan and also jealous. This was another time when her skating schedule kept her from socializing with her classmates. On the whole, that was fine by Madison. She loved skating and was willing to make the sacrifices necessary to progress as far as she could with competitions. All the same, Madison wished she had time to help Jordan get ready and go to the Halloween party. Madison counted Halloween celebrations out because regionals always fell the same week.

The sixth-period bell rang as Madison stood alone. Because of her training schedule, Madison was permitted to skip the last three periods every school day in order to get to the rink. As Madison rounded a corner, someone brushed past, knocking her off balance. Madison looked up and cringed.

"Why don't you watch where you are going?" Caitlin sneered.

"I...um...I," Madison stammered. Of all the girls in Madison's grade, she disliked Caitlin the most. Caitlin was a skater, too, and they had an ongoing rivalry—on and off the ice. Madison didn't understand Caitlin's need to measure her skating accomplishments against Madison's, but after years of dealing with it, Madison simply accepted it as a part of life. And Caitlin was also competing in Madison's group at regionals.

"On your way to practice, Madison? Good, you need it. I saw your footwork the other day," Caitlin arched an eyebrow, "and I doubt the caller will give you the level you're looking for. What are you expecting to get on it?"

"We choreographed it to get a level three," Madison said. "I'm sure it's fine. I know the rule. I have everything I need in there to get a high level."

"Well, we'll see. Your turns aren't clean enough, either. You may have all the elements, but that doesn't mean that the judges can tell what you're doing. They'll probably mark you down for them."

"Yeah, well, I'll work on my turns. I gotta go." Madison raced out to the parking lot. She could still hear Caitlin laughing after her.

Madison sank down on the curb with her head in her hands. She knew there was nothing wrong with her footwork—one of the best sequences in the rink and certainly better than Caitlin's. Actually, Madison was a much better all-around skater than Caitlin, but nobody at school knew that. Caitlin, as a popular girl surrounded by a clique of other popular people—walked around as if she were head and shoulders above Madison. Caitlin never admitted to friends that the two competed at the same level. She also insulted Madison's ability to their classmates. It frustrated Madison that Caitlin got to her. Madison had never stood up to her, never came back with the right words. And Madison especially hated the little voice inside that said, *What if she's right? Maybe you're not as good as everyone claims. Maybe Caitlin knows better.*

Madison tried to shake these thoughts as her mother's car pulled up. *Come on, Madison. Why are you doing this to yourself? You know what you can do. Don't let Caitlin get to you!* Madison silently pled.

"Hi, sweetie. How was school?"

"Fine." Madison climbed into the car. "Tyler asked Jordan to the Halloween fair on Friday."

"That's nice. She must be excited." Mrs. Albright paused, looking sideways at Madison. "Are you okay about not going to the fair?"

"I guess so. I'd like to go, but it's just impossible right now. Why let it bother me?" Madison reasoned.

"As long as you're okay with it. Did you pick up your assignments from your teachers?"

"Yes. Mrs. Williams and Mrs. Sharp were cool about giving me work ahead. Mrs. Matthews gave me a hard time, though. 'Going again? You had better get your priorities straight, young lady. Education is the key to your future!'" Madison mimicked her teacher's shrill voice, then huffed, "It's not like I've ever even missed an assignment. I think she gave me extra work just because I was leaving. I'm going to check with Jordan. If the rest of the class doesn't get the assignment, I'm not going to do it either."

Madison's mom laughed. They both knew she would do the assignment either way, but Madison needed to act defiant before she did as she was told.

"Madison, teachers are that way. They all think that their class is the most important. Mrs. Matthews just feels that her class should be your life's focus. Do what she asks and be really sweet. She'll warm up to you."

"I will," Madison sighed, "but it's not fair."

"Not everything is fair." Her mother's tone clued Madison that she was about to get a lecture about something—taking responsibility? Learning to deal with her teachers as a good lesson for the future? "Like how I was woken up this morning by doors slamming, for example."

Her mother's knowing look made Madison wince: *Shoot, I thought I got away with that. How does she know everything that happens at home?*

Madison blushed. "Sorry, Mom. I know Dylan is doing both you and me a favor by driving me to school, but he gets up so late. I'm always worried that I'll be late."

"That's understandable, Madison, but you have to learn to control your anger better. You can't just start yelling and slamming doors. I don't want such behavior becoming a habit."

"Okay. I already decided I would try harder not to get angry at him anymore. But could you *please* make him get up earlier? Buy him an alarm or something."

"Deal," her mom said, pulling up to the ice rink door. "I will be back for you in an hour and a half. Liz told me you don't need to skate a lot this week. Run your stuff and leave so you can rest."

Madison grabbed her skating bag and headed for the entrance. But she turned and blew her mom a kiss. "Love you," she mouthed as she went inside.

4

Feeling the Music

The cool of the ice rink washed over Madison, a welcome relief. The Midwest had experienced an unusually hot fall and the cold rink air was refreshing. She headed into the locker room to get dressed. Madison was glad to be the only one in the locker room; no one was on the ice yet, either. She had the place completely to herself. Once changed, she went out into the arena to warm up off-ice. Madison warmed up fifteen minutes before every practice and cooled down for thirty minutes after skating. She ran laps around the rink, followed with her Pilates mat positions, as her warm-up this afternoon. Madison tried not to rush, but she wanted to get on the ice before anyone else. Having the ice to herself was the best feeling in the world and Madison wanted to take advantage of that today. She was still alone as she stepped onto the ice. She put her music and guards down along the boards and skated across to the sound system. Besides being free to push without having to look out for anyone, another perk to skating alone was being able to play any music she wanted as loud as she wanted.

Her newest mix CD playing, she started gliding—slowly at first, just doing forward stroking, then backward, then cross strokes up and down the ice. Next Madison started warming up her upper body. Her arms floating high above her head, she circled them down to the ice in time with the music. She practiced classic arm movements as well as moves she'd had thought up herself. All the while, she let the music guide her.

15

Madison's favorite part of skating was letting the music flow through her whole body. She loved expressing everything she felt through skating. It was a special gift. Most competitors could perform the difficult jumps and spins, but not many could skate with enough emotion to move the audience and create a special connection.

"That was nice," Liz called. She was leaning against the boards watching Madison. Madison stopped what she was doing immediately. She might have a wonderful gift, but when asked to show it to people, she practically died of shyness.

"How long have you been there?" Madison asked sheepishly. She hadn't even noticed Liz come on to the ice. *How loud was I playing the music?* Madison wondered. She glided over to her coach to start her lesson.

"Long enough to see that you've been holding out on me. Madison, I knew you were musical, but I never knew you were *that* musical. Why don't you move like that doing your programs?"

"I'm just playing. I haven't practiced that stuff well enough yet to show it to anybody. I need some lessons on it."

"Lessons? Madison, that kind of emotion can't be taught. Either you have it or you don't. And you have it. It's time to show it off."

Madison didn't reply.

"All right. Do a five-minute warm-up and then we'll run your short. Then we'll do sections of your long."

Madison warmed up her spins first; her layback into Biellmann, her combination spin, and her back scratch—the fastest of her spins. Then she ran through her jumps: double flip, check; double Lutz combination, check; double axel, check. The last element she warmed up was her footwork. Today she focused on the deepness of her edges and the quality of the steps.

"Okay. Get in your starting position."

Madison skated to the center of the ice and struck her opening pose. As the first strains of *Romeo and Juliet* filled the ice arena, Madison closed her eyes and took a deep breath. Slowly she pushed off into the first element—the layback spin. Next, she went into her double Lutz combination. It was solid. About halfway through the program, Madison's mind went on autopilot. She stopped thinking about the elements; her muscle memory kicked in and she just went along for the ride. Once she had finished her clean program, she did a few laps and skated over to Liz.

"Not bad, girl. All the elements were there. Your footwork was especially strong. Yes, it was very good. In fact, it was one of your best run-throughs. But it's missing something, Madison. You're just going through the motions. The connection to the music isn't there. Even the way you just skated it, you showed more emotion than most skaters, but after watching you warm up, I know that you're not giving the programs your all. You have to let that ease of movement come through. Why don't you do that?"

"I don't know, Liz. I'll try," Madison replied quietly. Liz was right. Madison *did* hold back in the performance aspect of her program when she skated. In competition, Madison lacked the joy that she felt when she was skating alone. Madison knew that she would need to skate more musically, but she wished to blend in with the other skaters. If she skated with emotion, she would look different. Madison was reluctant to have everybody stare at her and thought, *What if they don't think I'm great but make fun of me?*

"Now run the middle section of your long. You've got the jumps. Let's see that musicality shine through."

"Cool." Madison's Spanish freeskate music started. She executed each element with precision but each section seemed identical.

"Good," Liz nodded, "but not great. You're still not putting expression into it. This is flamenco music—you have to look strong, passionate! Go home tonight and run through your program in front of your mirror. Watch your eyes, your shoulders, your hands. As you look, think about whether you are stretching your arms enough, opening your hands, and engaging your whole body. Will you do that?"

"Yes of course. I'm sorry Liz. I really thought I put more into it this time."

"I know. That's why it's good to watch yourself do it. Sometimes what you *feel* isn't always how it *looks.*"

Madison nodded. "Thank you for the lesson." Madison lifted her music out of the player, grabbed her guards from the boards, and skated off. Only as she left were the rest of the skaters arriving on the ice. Usually Madison stayed to skate with them, but today her workout ended early and for once, she was grateful. Liz had upset her and all she wanted to do was go home. *Why does she have to say that now? Right before regionals? Why can't I just skate before judges like I do when no one is watching?* Madison wondered as she took her skates off. She did a quick stretching routine and headed outside to look for her mom's car. Mrs. Albright was right on time. Madison gave her mom a short hello, then added that she was really tired and needed to sleep on the way home. Madison closed her eyes and rested her head back on the seat as sleep claimed her.

5

Mirror Image

"Madison," her mother shook her gently, "Wake up. We're home."

Madison groaned. She'd slept the whole way home. A thirty-minute nap usually refreshed her, but today she felt dull. She yawned, "I'm so tired I think I'll go to my room and sleep."

"I'm not surprised. This is a big week for you. It's probably taking more out of you than you realize. Why not sleep until dinner? Afterward you can do a little homework and turn in."

"Sounds good. I probably won't do any homework tonight, I'm so far ahead." Madison smiled as she remembered how her anxiety this past weekend had spurred her through a firestorm of homework.

Once in her bedroom with the door shut, she crossed with one stride to her bed and flopped down. Hands behind her head, she stared at the blank ceiling. She loved quiet time in her bedroom, daydreaming, listening to music, or writing about her day in her journal. Today Madison chose to daydream. She pictured being known around the world for her skating. It was a big dream, but Madison had a plan to make it happen, with the first step—winning regionals—in just three days.

She gazed at her dresser display of medals and trophies she'd earned in many competitions. How excited and nervous she was at age six, competing at her first event! As she finished that first event, she knew skating would be important in her life. Back then, she only knew how she loved her costume, the anticipation of preparing for each event, and of course the applause. Madison had placed second at that first competition, and the medal still hung proudly on her dresser. *Silver was fine then, but I want gold now*, she thought. And she was used to getting gold. Since that first competition, Madison had won almost every event she entered. She kept those competitions in perspective, though. She knew they were not qualifying events—those that drew the most talented skaters from all the states in the region and allowed medal winners to go on to U.S. Figure Skating's Junior Nationals Championship in December. It was fine to win the local events, but Madison wouldn't be truly satisfied until she stood atop a national or international podium. Regionals was her first big step in accomplishing her dream. If Madison finished in the top four among the hundred forty-five Intermediate Ladies at Upper Great Lakes, she'd compete at the national championship. If she skated well there, she could finish on the podium and receive a *national* medal—one of Madison's major goals.

She never discussed nationals—not even with Liz or her mother—for fear of jinxing it. Madison knew she was capable of winning regionals and moving onto Junior Nationals, provided that everything—technical elements, presentation, costume, music—worked for the actual event. In Madison's mind regionals was just a step toward her ultimate goal: winning at the Senior level by the time she was sixteen.

She'd never questioned that she would be successful once she was competing as a Senior Lady. Madison had several years to move through the Novice and Junior levels before finally hitting Senior. *Let's see, testing Novice by age thirteen, Junior by fifteen, and Senior by the time I'm sixteen!* Madison had calculated more than once. Time seemed to fly by and she needed to use every moment to reach these goals.

As tired as she'd been at first, thinking about her future *really* exhausted her. Madison had been struggling for a while to overcome her anxiety, live in the present, and enjoy the journey through the levels of skating. But she hadn't overcome her anxiousness. Eyes closed, she breathed deeply to clear her rogue thoughts. She pulled the covers up to her ears. Before long, she was fast asleep.

Madison awoke several hours later. To get her bearings, she looked out the window. It was already dark outside. *Wow, I must have really been tired*, Madison thought, shaking her head. She heard a low rumble and looked down at her stomach. How long since she'd had lunch? Madison made her way toward the kitchen. Dinner was already over. Maybe she could scrounge up leftovers. She passed Dylan's room quietly, although his music blared into the hall. He hummed, stopping and starting the music over and over. He was playing his own music again. Dylan was always trying to compose, and although she never told him, he was pretty good. Their parents always joked that both kids in the family would become famous. Madison hoped that when she became a major competitor, Dylan would compose a song for her program. Madison had visions of older versions of herself and her musical brother creating a skating show together. Their show would be a hit! *You're getting too far ahead of yourself*, Madison scolded as she explored the fridge. But it never hurt to dream big; it inspired her and helped push her harder on the ice.

Madison did not have to look far for food. In the center of the kitchen table a plate was laid out. The plate was covered with leftovers—chicken, corn, and brown rice with peppers; very healthy and tasty. She found the small note beside the plate and read:

Hi, sweetheart! I thought it was more important for you to sleep rather than eat with us. Of course, we missed you at the dinner table, but you have a big event to get ready for, so we understand. I made you a plate! Enjoy!

Love,

Mom

Madison both smiled and rolled her eyes. She loved her mom to show her special care like this, but Mom always worried whether she felt left out because of her skating. Her mom obsessed about it! Mrs. Albright repeatedly went out of her way to make sure that Madison saw herself as part of a family who missed her when she wasn't with them. Notes like this helped Madison feel like she belonged.

It was 9:15 when she finished eating. She still had Liz's assignment to complete, but she wanted to wait until everyone was asleep before she used the big mirror in the hallway to practice expression.

Madison was just stacking her dishes when her dad entered the kitchen.

"Hey, Maddie, how was your day?"

"Oh fine. Practice was good. Then I came home and slept. I slept most of the day, actually. I was so tired."

"That's what Mom said, but I see you've eaten. You going back to sleep?"

"Later. I have to work on this thing for Liz." As soon as she said it, Madison regretted it. Now her dad would want to know what "this thing" was and ask to watch. And she really wanted to do this in private.

"What thing?"

"Practicing my program in the mirror. I'm supposed to work on my expression."

"Always working," her father said. "Hey, can I watch? I may not be the best dancer in the world, but I know what looks good. I could help." Mr. Albright looked hopeful. He worked a lot and they didn't have much time together. He constantly looked for ways to be involved with her and stay current with Madison's life. Madison especially loved that about her dad and wanted to spend time with him, but not *this* time.

"No, Dad. I don't think so. I need to do this by myself." Madison bit her lip as her dad's face registered hurt and disappointment.

"Okay, honey. Whatever you need to do to skate your best." He kissed her forehead. "You'll do great, I'm sure. Don't stay up too late."

"Night." She felt guilty for not letting her father watch her. But tonight was no different. She never wanted her dad or her friends to see her practice or compete. It was no problem to skate in front of people she didn't know, but when she performed before the people close to her, she completely froze. Lots of skaters were like that, which Madison often reminded her family, but she saw that it bothered them not to come to the rink.

Only her mother watched her skate and that was because Mrs. Albright had insisted on it. Her argument was that if she spent so much time driving Madison to practice, managing travel to events, and arranging costume fittings, she should at least be allowed to watch lessons and practice. After much bickering, Madison had finally given in. The first few times her mother had watched, Madison was distracted, but eventually she got used to it. Now her mom watched every competition and Madison didn't mind. But she was the only family member or friend Madison allowed to see her skate.

Madison slowly climbed upstairs and saw that all the bedroom doors were closed, but light was streaming from under them. She knew her mom would watch the news while her dad would finish off paperwork, but before long it would be lights off. As usual, Dylan was still playing around with his music. So Madison returned to her bedroom and pulled her journal out from its hiding place under her nightstand. She tried to journal every night before bed to let go of all the day's events. Sometimes she made lists of what to do the following day.

October 14

I'm waiting till everyone goes to bed to go to the hallway mirror and practice my program. It's silly, but I don't want my family to see me trying the moves on the floor. They'd spook me! Dad wanted to help, but I wouldn't let him. He was disappointed, but I have to do what makes me feel comfortable, right? He probably has a lot of work to do, anyway.

Practice was good. I skated a clean short and all of my sections were clean, too. But Liz said that I was not expressing myself much. She snuck into the rink while I was warming up and saw me skating to the music I really like. She told me I don't skate that freely in my program. I didn't know that I skated any differently once my competition music came on! How can I fix my presentation before regionals? Will it mess up my chances to win? Everything else is good, except that Caitlin came up to me today and tried to psych me out before practice. It worked for a while, but I tried not to let it affect me. She criticized my footwork, but Liz said that I did it especially well today. That shows Caitlin!

Oh yeah, and Tyler asked Jordan to the Halloween fair. So she finally has a date with him after years of crushing on him! Good for her. I'm going to help her pick out her outfit. Too bad I can't be there to see her wear it.

After finishing her journal entry, Madison peaked out into the hallway to see that the only light was coming from under Dylan's door. His music was so soft she knew he had settled in for the night. Now was the perfect time to see how she could transfer the emotion from her warm-up into her performance.

Watching her reflection, Madison struck the opening pose of her short program. She stood with her feet parallel, one toe pointed and her body tilted left. Her arms extended gently out in front of her. Her program music had a slow tempo, so her opening pose should convey elegance. She studied her image and tried to stretch her arms a little longer and point her toe even more. Madison wanted even the person sitting farthest from the ice to see every detail and shape that her body created.

After an hour, Madison was tired, but happy with herself; she had not grown self-conscious once. She thought, *Yes! If I keep this level of confidence, I'm sure I'll skate well at regionals.* As she climbed into bed, she looked forward to getting on the ice the next day to show what she could do.

chapter

6

Morning Announcements

Instead of waiting until the last minute to wake Dylan, Madison began nudging him awake at seven thirty. It took almost fifteen minutes and several pillows thrown (gently) at his head to wake him, but Madison and her brother left for school with time to spare. Dylan grumbled, but a new routine had begun. It was Madison's plan to get Dylan up a little earlier each day so they both had time to eat breakfast and avoid the last minute rush.

The bell rang signaling for homeroom to start. As Madison slid into her seat, Mrs. Mulberry began taking attendance. "Abbott, Jason; Ackerman, Amanda; Albright, Madison; Bergens, Camyrn…." She continued down the list. Everyone was present today. Before Madison could read her teacher's look, she turned and said, "Quiet, please…settle down. The announcements are starting. Something involves one of you." Mrs. Mulberry sighed and sat behind her enormous wooden desk. She flipped open the day's agenda, carefully took off her glasses, and set them aside.

The loudspeaker crackled, and then the voice of a young girl began leading the pledge of allegiance.

"Stand up," barked Mrs. Mulberry. "Put your hands on your hearts. You are paying tribute to your country."

The class stood up and pushed in their chairs, scraping them loudly on the bare floor. Mrs. Mulberry groaned and slapped her hand to her head. After the pledge, the class sat down to hear the announcements.

Finally, the last announcement blared, "And good luck to Caitlin Jackson and Madison Albright at the Upper Great

Lakes Regional figure skating championships this weekend in Minnesota. We're sure you will make us very proud." There was more crackling, and then the loudspeaker shut off. Madison thought she would die from embarrassment. She had not planned to tell her classmates about the competition. Half of them didn't even know she was a skater. She spotted Jordan, who smiled at her. Suddenly, Madison felt a tap on her shoulder. She turned around to see Peter, the boy who sat behind her, staring at her.

"You're a figure skater? I had no idea. Like, what kind of tricks can you do? Triple jumps, backflips?"

Madison turned two shades of red. Peter had never spoken to her. She had been in school with him since kindergarten and now, because of this announcement, he suddenly felt the need to talk to her?

"Um, I can do a few triples, yeah. No backflips, though. Not yet, anyway."

"Cool. Are you gonna go to the Olympics? I mean could you, like, soon?"

Madison laughed silently. This was the first question people always asked when they realized that she was a figure skater. It was the toughest one to answer, too. If you said you were going someday, you put an awful lot of pressure on yourself, plus promised something that was not really under your control. However, if you said you weren't going, people always seemed a tad disappointed and seemed to decide you must not be good enough to make the Olympic Team. Madison weighed the response of each answer in her head before saying, "I'm trying. I can't guess who will make it because so many things affect who becomes a champion. But if I keep working like I am now, I think I have a pretty good shot of making the Olympics someday."

"Wow. When I see you on TV, I'll point to you and tell everybody that I know you and I sat behind you in middle school."

"Sure," Madison said. She had given the answer she always gave to the Olympics question and Peter seemed to enjoy her response. After all, he was going to look for her on TV someday. Before Peter could ask another question, the bell rang to signal second period. Madison shot like a rocket out of her seat.

"Maddie," Jordan called as she pushed her way through the throng of students heading out the door, "Wait!"

Madison stopped just long enough to grab Jordan by the hand and push her through the door.

The pair raced through the hallway amid smiles and good luck wishes, entering their second-period classroom before anyone else.

"What was that about?" Jordan panted, slumping down in her seat. "Aren't you excited that they announced your name this morning? You act like it's the worst thing in the world."

"It is," Madison wailed. "Now everyone knows that I'm competing this weekend."

"So? Now you have the class sending you good wishes and support. That's not so bad."

Madison shook her head. "Jordan, you don't understand. It would have been better if the announcement were made next Monday—after the competition. That way people would only know if I do well."

"Won't you, though? I mean, you train all the time and you said your coach thinks you could win."

"Yes, but I was hoping to avoid telling anyone now. Monday everyone will ask me how I did. If I medal, that's one thing, but if I don't skate well, what will people think?"

"They're going to think that maybe you had an off day or the judging wasn't fair or something," Jordan offered.

Madison looked unconvinced.

"Look," Jordan continued, "I don't think that people will make as big of a deal about it as you think. They'll just think it's cool that you skate and go to these competitions. I do. And when they ask about it, they're just curious. I don't think they want to pry into your life just to criticize you. Well, some people might." Jordan paused and threw a dirty glance at Caitlin and her posse.

"Now they," Jordan said, pointing at Caitlin's group, "might be ones to watch out for, but how you do at regionals doesn't change anything. Caitlin will always try to find something mean to say about you. Other kids will be on your side."

29

"Yeah, but it's more than Caitlin. Peter in homeroom talked to me for the first time today because of the announcement."

"See? He's cute, too. Maybe he'll take you to one of the dances coming up." Jordan winked at her with a devilish grin.

"Hey, let's not push it," Madison laughed. "He was nice, I guess."

By now, their classmates had taken their seats and the teacher was taking roll. She then used the white board to write today's new math formulas. Madison let her mind wander. She first thought of Jordan's suggestion that there might be a "date" with Peter in her future. Madison was not really big on the idea. She was not particularly boy crazy, and she had too much else going on to try to make interesting conversation with a boy. That was Jordan, though. Since the school year began, Jordan had been absolutely fascinated with boys and dating. Jordan had decided that this was the year she was going to talk to Tyler and spend time with him. She went after what she wanted and usually got it. Tyler was no exception. It helped that Jordan was extremely outgoing and always unafraid to throw herself into the next available activity.

Madison spotted Caitlin, who sat legs crossed and elbows resting on the desk. She looked like she might fall asleep. The other members of her clique were sitting with rapt attention, vigorously taking notes. Caitlin knew that if she fell asleep one of her friends would explain what she'd missed. Madison surveyed the group. All four of them had a similar look: hair long and straight, a fashionable headband fastened around the crown of their heads, light pink or purple eye shadow, and a shiny lip gloss. Despite their school uniforms, Caitlin and her friends stood out. They always wore the right amount of jewelry that sparkled just so against the stark white uniform shirt. Their shoes always were the latest style, and they carried themselves as if they were walking down a runway instead of the hallway. Caitlin formed this clique at the beginning of middle school, and every girl knew where she stood in the eyes of the four popular girls. Madison was not high on the list. Jordan was much higher, but she'd never abandoned Madison. When Madison needed a friend, Jordan was there.

As much as Madison despised Caitlin and the way her rival treated her, Madison secretly wanted to be a tiny bit like her. She wished she could carry off the uniform with such style and walk around as if she didn't have a care in the world—to ooze self-assurance. Madison wondered, *What makes some people naturally confident, while I have a hard time seeing myself as someone special?*

"Gosh, I thought she'd never stop talking," Jordan muttered under her breath as class ended. "Are you lucky to be missing three days of that or what?"

They walked to English class and sat down. Madison took out her copy of *Tom Sawyer* to review the chapter summaries due today. English passed by slowly and soon Madison was on to fourth period—halfway through her day. In social studies the class was studying ancient Egypt, a subject Madison thoroughly enjoyed, which helped time fly.

As the school day passed, Madison was overwhelmed by well-wishers asking about her skating. She grew more weary each time. Madison massaged her temples and cursed the announcement. Like she didn't have enough to worry about already!

7

Caitlin's Scheme

Madison walked into the rink just after one that afternoon. The familiarity of the ice and its surroundings were comforting. She was the first person to arrive for the afternoon sessions and the rink was now a quiet retreat where she could unwind. The confidence boost she'd gained from improving her expression in the mirror carried over into today. Warm relief spread over Madison; her worries dissipated as she warmed up her footwork. Instead of doubting whether each rocker, counter, and bracket was done with enough edge quality and precision, Madison felt light on her feet. Each turn erupted from a place so deep inside her that she was elated. After ten blissful minutes of private ice, Liz appeared, followed by several young skaters who would also be competing this weekend. Madison circled one more lap and then came to her coach.

"How's it going?" Liz asked.

"Good! I feel great today," Madison said brightly.

"That's nice to hear. Did you do what I asked last night?" Liz questioned sternly. She expected her students to follow her instructions to a tee and scolded them if they did not.

"Yes. I waited until everyone was asleep, but I did both the short and long. At first it was hard to watch myself, but by the end I could and I think it helped a lot."

Liz smiled with satisfaction. "All right. I'm going to take Caitlin first. I'll come for you in half an hour. Warm everything up and be ready to run your long."

Madison nodded and turned to skate away thinking, *I usually have first lesson; how odd that Liz switched her time today.* Nevertheless, practice was great so far and Madison wasn't going to let the tiniest thing bother her. Caitlin was probably just trying to mess with Madison's routine. *Not a very good way to try to psych me out,* Madison thought. *I'm in way too good a mood.* Madison was in control, allowing nothing to bother her. She began skating faster, heading into the center to spin. *Nothing is going to get...*BAM! Her body reeled as she sprawled on the ice. She was dazed for a moment, having the wind knocked out of her. She blinked a few times, trying to remember what had happened right before she landed on the ice. Suddenly she heard a whizzing sound and raised her head a few more inches to see where it was coming from. It was Liz skating over to her furiously.

"Maddie! Are you hurt? Can you stand?" Liz was frantically bending over her and checking whether different body parts were intact.

Madison stood up slowly. "I'm fine, I think. What happened exactly?"

"I didn't see," Liz said. "I turned to put Caitlin's music on and heard a thud, and you were down. Did anyone see what happened?" Liz addressed the small crowd of girls that had gathered. Most of the girls kept their eyes down, afraid to make eye contact. A few girls fidgeted with their hair or sweaters. Finally, one girl, with a long blonde braid, raised her hand.

"Carly?" Liz pointed at her.

The little girl gasped, but looked up and locked eyes with Liz. It was obvious that Carly felt as if she were being stared down.

"Well, Madison was going into the spin circle." She paused, and Madison nodded reassurance. Carly took another deep breath and continued, "Right as she was going to step into the spin, someone came and cut her off, trying to blade her." Carly dropped her gaze.

Liz raised an eyebrow. "Don't be ridiculous, Carly. No one in this rink would deliberately try to hurt another skater. I do not teach that type of sportsmanship here."

Carly bit her lip and Madison could see her start to shake. She was crying. Despite her own shakiness, Madison sympathized with Carly's reluctance to cross Liz.

"I think we've spent enough time on this. Let's get back to work," Liz said curtly.

"Wait," Madison spoke up. If Carly could help her, she could most certainly help Carly. "Did anyone else see what happened?" She scanned the remaining group of skaters.

"Madison," Liz warned.

"I did, actually." Another skater, Angela, raised her head bravely. "Carly is right. Someone did try to blade Madison. You always tell us to keep a safe distance between us, but this person came really close to Madison, looking right at her. She must have been trying to hurt her."

Liz cleared her throat. "And who, pray tell, is this *someone* who tried to hurt Madison?"

Silence. No one wanted to look like the tattletale or, worse, tell the truth and have Liz doubt her. For her students Liz's respect was everything. Finally, Carly stepped forward again.

"I think it was Caitlin." She said quietly.

"You think or you *know*?" Liz snapped

"I know." The other skaters looked around. Caitlin was gone.

"Where is she?" Madison asked. "I don't think I even saw her come to the circle in the first place."

The girls remained still and silent as Liz glared at them. "Enough drama for one day. I will speak to Caitlin about it later. Go back to practice."

The girls skated off into small groups, grumbling that their teacher seemed angry with them and not with Caitlin.

Madison still had not moved. Liz turned back to face her. "You sure you're all right? I don't see any blood. Does anything hurt?"

"My hip is a little sore, but other than that, I'm fine."

"Good. Why would the girls say that Caitlin would try to blade you?"

Madison shrugged. "Because she probably did. She doesn't like me very much."

"You know I don't tolerate that type of behavior. You are my best skater, Madison, and I expect you to set a good example for the younger students. A rivalry on this scale is not the way to do that. Honestly, I expected more from you."

Madison's jaw dropped in shock. "Me?" she asked. "I'm the one knocked down!"

"Yes, but if you weren't egging Caitlin on, it would never have gotten to this point. Here she comes now. I will still see you in half an hour."

With that, Liz skated to Caitlin. Madison saw Liz questioning Caitlin, whose eyes grew round and whose expression remained innocent. Madison blinked away resentful tears. Caitlin would get out of this—even make it look like Madison was in the wrong.

Liz put her arm around Caitlin, who then skated off without a care to start jumping. Madison laughed sarcastically and wiped her eyes in frustration, thinking *Caitlin got the best of me again.* But the day wasn't over. Madison decided to skate so well during her lesson she'd prove she was the better skater.

"Wow, Madison. Anger must motivate you," Liz said after the lesson.

"I wasn't angry," Madison lied. "I just used what I learned last night." That was only half true.

"You looked angry to me. Well, whatever the reason for the good work, keep it up. Cool down now and I will see you here tomorrow before you leave."

"Thanks for the lesson." Madison exited the ice feeling a little smug. Liz had been angry with her as the session began, but Madison had turned her mood around by skating well. Quite a feat; only the best programs could improve Liz's mood. In the end, Caitlin had not ruined Madison's day after all. She was skating with an ease that she'd lacked for quite a while.

I can handle Caitlin now. Anything she throws at me, Madison thought proudly. She was finishing her stretching routine as Carly came through the door.

"Maddie, was it wrong of me to say that Caitlin tried to blade you? She did, you know."

"No, Carly, it was a brave thing you did. Thank you."

"I don't think Liz was too happy."

"She'll get over it. She just doesn't like the idea that such bad feelings could happen among her students. She's not mad at you, believe me."

"I hope not. I just wanted her to know the truth."

"It's for the best. Thanks again. Good luck this weekend."

Carly smiled. "Thanks. You too."

Madison walked out, keeping her head down. She didn't want to meet anyone who would ask questions. Luckily, her mother's car sat at the entrance and Madison could jump right in.

"How was…?"

"Don't ask." Madison pulled her hood over her head. "The skating was great, but I hate some skaters right now."

"Oh, no. In-house fighting?"

"I said, don't ask," Madison whined and waited for her mother's reprimand. But it didn't come.

Instead, she said, "Tell me later if you want. Just know if anyone's giving you a hard time, you can talk to me about it. I'm here to listen."

"I know. Right now I just want to be left alone."

"Do you want me to call and tell Jordan that you can't come over now?"

"No!" Madison sat up. "Her room is one place I want to be."

At least at Jordan's she could regain some sense of everyday life. The blading incident was too insane for Madison to wrap her head around.

A few minutes later Madison was ringing Jordan's doorbell. When Jordan opened the door, Madison threw her arms around her.

"Nice to see you too," Jordan laughed. She studied Madison's face. "What happened?" She pulled Madison inside.

"You'll never believe it!"

They went upstairs to Jordan's awesome bedroom. It matched her personality perfectly: bright and cheerful. They jumped up on Jordan's bed, with its pink and yellow tie-dye bedspread. Jordan grabbed a huge, fluffy pillow to rest on and threw Madison a matching one.

"Talk," Jordan instructed.

After Madison described the blading, she was fuming again. Then she sighed. "I think we underestimated just *how much* Caitlin really hates me. If she'd hurt me worse I could've had to withdraw from regionals. I was lucky that she wasn't skating close enough to do serious damage—*really* lucky."

Jordan didn't understand much about skating or how much damage a jealous skater could inflict with her skate blade or toepick, but she hung on Madison's every word.

"But what's worse," Madison continued, "is that when Caitlin denied the whole thing, Liz got mad at *me*. She said I was egging Caitlin on. Liz took her side. She even gave Caitlin a hug after they talked about what happened."

Jordan scoffed, "That's ridiculous. If I were you, I would march up and tell Liz about all the grief Caitlin has given you. You shouldn't be the one who is in trouble."

"I know, but it will probably blow over fast. All of us have tomorrow's trip to get past it. Bringing it up again will just cause more trouble."

"Caitlin always tries to make you look bad, and right now she's doing a great job of it."

"The girls at the rink know what really happened," Madison said defensively.

"But Liz doesn't. And her opinion is the one that really matters."

"You're right. Maybe I'll discuss it after regionals. Right now I just want to focus on the actual event," Madison smiled. "And I also want to focus on what you'll wear Friday night."

Madison was a whiz at changing the subject when it made her uncomfortable. Jordan nodded and decided to let her friend have her way. Besides, she did need Madison's help in deciding what to wear to the fair, and Madison was leaving tomorrow.

Jordan's closet revealed piles of folded shirts and sweaters in the latest styles, plus hangers of jeans, skirts, pants, and coats. Jordan loved clothes almost as much as she loved boys. When she was not obsessing about which boy she liked, she obsessed about the next fashion trend.

Madison didn't have nearly this large a wardrobe. She didn't have time to shop for clothes or that many places to wear them. Gazing at the many outfit possibilities, Madison thought, *Even though I have such an active and outgoing friend, I'm not very outgoing myself.* Jordan frequently invited Madison to go to the movies or the mall to hang out with friends, but Madison usually found a way out of going. She pondered, *Why do I do that? I want to go out, but I feel awkward with Jordan's friends. They might not like me for myself and just think of me as a skater who does everything alone.* Madison decided she was more comfortable just hanging out with Jordan or Jillian, the one other friend she'd had since she was very young.

"So," she heard Jordan announce, "outfit number one."

Jordan threw a jean skirt on the bed over black leggings. She then pulled out a long-sleeved silk tee and new studded vest to top it off.

"Outfit number two." A pair of jeans with a very simple blue sweater landed next to the first selection. Jordan tossed the last outfit onto the bed without any fanfare—a black skirt with a light pink tank. Madison thought the outfit looked fine on the bed, but the top seemed too tight and the skirt too short for a school event. Madison compared the outfits on the bed carefully for a few moments and slowly leaned over and picked up the first one.

"This one," She said. "Definitely." She didn't give Jordan time to ask why. "Because it is totally you. The jeans and the sweater look like you are trying to be boring and simple— which you are *not*—and the skirt and tank top look like you are trying too hard. The jean skirt with the tee is perfect: fun but not over the top and certainly not boring."

Jordan laughed, "Wow, I thought we were going to take a lot longer. Can I at least try it on for you, so you can help me with the shoes and hair stuff?"

Madison nodded. Jordan went to her bathroom to change and emerged looking very spunky.

"I like it," Jordan enthused. 'It's everything I wanted. Flirty, yet sophisticated. Edgy but not too edgy."

"I agree, You look great. You'll have to take lots of pictures for me."

"For sure," Jordan promised, trying on shoes. The girls eventually decided to pair the outfit with ankle-high boots. Jordan would wear her hair down, curled.

Madison yawned, "Well, I think my work here is done. I should get home and pack. I have to be on the ice really early tomorrow and then we leave for Minnesota."

Madison phoned her mom to pick her up.

"Are you jittery about competing?" Jordan asked.

"Yes. I mean I have been for the last several weeks, but I was okay today. I felt ready, you know?"

"You're going to win. I know you are," Jordan said proudly.

"Don't jinx it! I'm trying not to think about that part. I really have to win if I want to stay on my track and...I won't know what to do if that doesn't happen."

"Just go there and enjoy Minnesota—if there is anything to do in Minnesota besides Mall of America." The girls laughed. "And you'll have the satisfaction of whipping Caitlin's butt."

"That's true," Madison agreed.

Even if Madison skated badly she would probably beat Caitlin. It would be a small consolation, but it would be something.

"Madison, your mom is here," Jordan's mother called from downstairs.

"Coming." Madison headed for the door.

"Thanks for helping me with my outfit. Good luck this weekend." Jordan hugged her. "And remember, don't let people walk all over you. This is your competition, your chance to show what you can do. Don't let Caitlin get the best of you."

Madison thanked Jordan's mom for having her over and soon she was back in her own room, packing. Butterflies flitted around her stomach as she added her costumes. These butterflies were caused by anticipation and excitement: *I just can't wait to get to Minnesota and get the competition going.* She heard a knock as her mom stepped inside.

"I'm packed. Do you need any help, Maddie?"

"Yes. Could you take my skates and costumes downstairs? I am almost done. I don't need much for this trip."

"Hmm. Did you pack your curler?"

"Yes."

"Hairspray?"

"Yes."

"Warm-up clothes?"

"Yes, Mom, I know how to pack myself."

"You seemed distracted on the way home. I want to make sure everything is good."

"It is. I was upset earlier, but I'm fine now. Jordan is right. This is my competition and I can't let anyone interfere with that."

"If you ever want to talk about it...."

"Mom, I'm fine," Madison snapped. "Talking just makes things worse."

"Okay, okay. Tomorrow we need to be out of here by six forty-five so you can skate for an hour before we drive. So get to bed."

"I will."

Mrs. Albright came over and gave her daughter a kiss. "You're going to do great, honey. I'm proud of you no matter what place you get. You're working so hard."

"Thanks." Madison wiggled out of her mom's embrace. "I have to get to bed."

"Good night—hey," her mom paused in the doorway, "have you thought about what kind of dog you want?"

"Not really. I want to see what happens first."

Mom nodded. "Night, sweetie." With that, she closed the door.

Madison jumped on her bed and covered her head with a pillow. She let out a low scream. Just when she thought the pressure was off, there was some new worry. As she got into bed, she replayed visions of today's practice in her mind. *It's gonna be fine. I'm gonna do great*, Madison thought, drifting to sleep.

8

A Shaky Practice

Six o'clock came too early for Madison on Wednesday morning. Half asleep, she dressed and helped her mom load their luggage into the car. She remained groggy when she said good-bye to her father and Dylan. Mrs. Albright had insisted that both get up to see her off and wish her luck.

Madison didn't see much point in getting her brother out of bed this early. Dylan was sleeping standing up; he only mumbled, "Don't blow it." Her dad managed to wake up enough to give her a tight hug and wish her all the best. As the car left the driveway, Madison looked behind her one last time. Her dad was waving and Dylan was rocking back and forth on his heels trying to stay awake. The car rounded the corner, and she saw her family turn and go back inside the house. *How lucky to be them,* she thought. *They don't have to worry about performing. They just get to go about their everyday lives.* Madison nestled herself into the backseat and pulled the blanket in tight around her.

Her mom peered into the rearview mirror. "Good. You should sleep. I'll wake you when we get to the rink. You know, honey, I was thinking, I might come in to watch. Is that okay with you? I mean, I'll watch the competition anyway. What difference will watching practice make?"

Madison hesitated. "Um, I guess so. It's so early, it might not be my best skate. Are you sure you want to see that? You could just wait until we get to Minnesota." *Please*, Madison thought to herself. Having Mom watch a practice was almost

43

as nerve-wracking as having Dad see it, and this morning she really didn't need more grief.

"It's making you nervous. I will wait until Minnesota. You just seem more jumpy than usual, and I'm trying to be supportive."

"I'm not any more nervous today. You can come in if you want to. Really, it's okay." Madison hoped her answer would satisfy her mother and that she would be content to sit in the lobby until Madison finished. Instead of continuing the conversation, her mother fell silent and turned up the car radio. Madison drifted off to sleep until they reached the rink.

The parking lot was full. Madison knew the ice would be packed—and even hazardous—with skaters trying to work in a last-minute practice session before regionals. She was geared up to avoid collisions.

And crowded it was: skaters, coaches, and mothers everywhere. Some were frantically making last-minute costume adjustments, others were stretching, and some were warming up. Madison approached the locker room putting her iPod on. She warmed up off-ice in her own little world. Listening to music, she became oblivious to distractions and could keep her head clear. She laced her skates up twenty minutes later and headed to the freshly made ice.

"Morning, Bryan," Madison said to the Zamboni driver she knew well. "How's it going?"

Bryan looked up from sweeping the ice. The two had developed a friendship over the years. Bryan, who played on a local hockey team, had only been a teenager when Madison had started skating at Arctic Circle and he was now well into his twenties.

"This is always a fun week for me, though," he grinned. "Regionals week all of us Zamboni drivers place bets to see how many girls are going to cry before each day is over. I'm winning. I bet that ten would cry yesterday and I counted at least eleven. No one else guessed that many."

Madison laughed. Regionals week was stressful, and many competitors broke down during the days prior to the event. For most skaters it was their one chance to progress from the region to qualify nationally. For some it was their only competition of the year.

"That's because you've been here the longest of anyone. You've seen us all go through this every year!" Madison joked back.

"True. But you are one of the few that I have not seen lose yet."

"*Yet* is the key word," Madison replied with a smile.

"Oh, you'll be fine. I know you. You're a tough competitor."

"Thanks, but hold off on any big bets for this event."

"Have a good skate."

Madison felt at ease as she stroked her first lap. She shared the ice with fourteen other skaters, but she could have been out there alone, she was so focused. Liz was instructing Carly. Madison smiled, glad that the rift had apparently been mended between coach and student. That reassured Madison that she was right to let the blading incident blow over. She was only to skate an hour this morning to run through her programs, then travel to Minnesota. Her short program went off without a hitch. She landed the double axel beautifully and went on to do yet another clean program. It was not her best by any means, but she didn't need to peak until Friday morning—the day of her short program in competition. Madison took a short breather and prepared to run her long.

She was tired; the weight of yesterday's events had taken its toll. But she was determined to fight through it. She could rest as soon as she got off the ice; right now, she had a job to do. Muscle memory took over as the Spanish music filled the rink. Halfway through the program, Madison was skating with assurance. Everything flowed. She was just coming out of her spiral sequence when she spotted her mom enter the bleachers. A slight twinge struck her stomach and Madison tried to concentrate.

Her triple toe was next and she really wanted to nail it. She did her best to push all thoughts out of her head as she entered the jump. On her way down it was as if Madison forgot how to land. She hit the ice with a loud thud. She sat there for a second, dazed. She hadn't fallen in a long time on that jump. *Keep going,* her inner voice said, and Madison quickly stood and found where to pick up the program. She landed her double Lutz-double loop combination, though not solidly. She went into her final combination spin, which was shaky as well. She even fell out of the last element and barely ended on time. As she held her final position, she saw Liz watching her, wearing a puzzled expression. Madison was confused, too. *Why does mom's presence throw me?* she wondered, because indeed it had. She had lost her concentration—something rare for Madison. She skated laps as her cool-down, and when she passed the spot where her mother had been sitting, it was empty. Madison quickly ran through her triple toe one more time. She landed it, but not well.

"Madison," Liz called.

Madison could tell from her look that Liz was still upset about yesterday. Madison also knew Liz would try to hide that in order to focus on today's events.

"It was a good short. I saw the end of the long. Not your best."

Madison sighed deeply. Liz put her arm around her. "Hey, it's okay. It's better, actually. You don't have to give the best performance today. I'd rather you work the kinks out now and be ready to go when the time is right. So don't beat yourself up about one missed jump."

"My mom made me nervous. That's never happened before," Madison confessed.

"If she makes you nervous, ask her not to watch. If you can get over it, then she can. That is something you two can decide. I am sure your mom wants to head up to Minnesota now, so get changed. It's a long drive. I am catching a flight later this evening. Make sure you rest in the car and have a good dinner. Get a good night's sleep. You don't practice until later in the day tomorrow, but I want you raring to go by then."

"Thanks. I'll, um, see you tomorrow."

"Maddie, I mean it," Liz said gently but firmly. "It's okay. You're ready."

"I know."

In the locker room another disaster awaited her. Caitlin sat lacing up her skates. Her eyes narrowed at Madison. Trouble was brewing.

"Madison," Caitlin blasted. A few other girls in the locker room looked up. "Why did you accuse me of trying to blade you? You know I'd never do that."

"I didn't accuse you. It happened so fast I'm not sure who it was or what happened."

"Are you accusing me now, then?" Caitlin's voice rose a few more octaves. Now everyone watched their exchange.

"Caitlin, stop. I don't have time for this. We both know what happened, but it's over. Let's move on."

"That's what someone with a guilty conscience would say. You don't admit that you're making up nasty rumors about me?" Caitlin sneered.

"I think that guilty someone is you." Madison shot back. She whisked up her bag and walked out of the room, leaving Caitlin stunned and speechless. Madison was seething, *Jordan was right. This has to stop. Caitlin is ruining my reputation. She's hurting me but making it look like I'm on her case.* She slammed her skates into her bag and ripped the main door open. She slammed her mom's car door, too.

"Maddie, what's wrong?"

"Mom? We need to talk."

9

Minnesota Bound

Several hours and two states later, Madison had filled her mother in on everything that had been going on with Caitlin. Naturally, her mother was furious, partly because of what Caitlin had done but also because Madison hadn't told her about it sooner.

"We should inform Liz about this. You are getting in trouble for something that is not your fault. You don't need that stress heading into regionals."

"No, Mom," Madison protested. "Please. It's only going to be worse if you say something. Then it will look like I put you up to it and that I'm on the defensive. I want to handle this on my own."

"Handling a mean girl is one thing," her mother said firmly, "but handling someone who really tried to hurt you—I want to step in about that."

"Come on. Regionals will be over in two days. Then we can tell Liz if you think we should. I don't want to have to worry that you are going to say something to her, because that could cause more problems for me."

"I don't see how being a concerned parent will cause you problems."

"Trust me—Liz wants us to manage our relationships on our own. If I involve you, it's just going to become a bigger deal. Please don't say anything. For me?" Madison gave her mother a puppy face.

"Ahh, fine. I will not say anything this week. But if I see anything suspicious, anything that looks like this girl is trying to hurt you, I'm going straight to Liz."

"Fine. But you won't see anything. Every minute we are on practice ice someone is watching us. Caitlin won't try anything." Madison was trying to reassure herself more than her mother. Caitlin had almost gotten away with blading her and making it look like Madison had fallen by herself. Madison wasn't sure that next time Caitlin wouldn't get away with it.

"How 'bout a rest stop?" her mother asked.

"How close are we?"

"Oh, I'd say we've got another two hours."

"Great," Madison groaned.

In the rest stop washroom she splashed cold water on her face. Doubts had crept into her head during the drive. Glancing at her image in the mirror, she looked pale and edgy. Could her restlessness be due to the long drive, or was it something else? Talking about Caitlin always made her nervous. Plus, approaching Minnesota increased her anxiousness.

After waiting for regionals all these months, she was tempted to ask her mother to turn the car around and head home. *Let's see,* she rattled off, *I'm nervous about mom watching; concerned about Caitlin doing something to throw me off; and worried about disappointing friends and spectators.* Most of all, she was worried about not reaching her goal to progress to nationals.

Great. I'm not even at the competition yet and I've already psyched myself out so badly I want to go home. Get it together, Madison! The young skater turned away from her mirror image. She took a deep breath, pulled herself up to her full height, and marched out the door.

"I'm ready, mom. Let's go," Madison announced. She was determined to appear casual. Her mother slid into the driver's seat.

"Bossy, bossy," her mother joked and they were on the road once more.

Upon their arrival at their Minnesota hotel, the afternoon sun was high and it was hot.

"It's the end of October!" Madison exclaimed. 'It should be cold, no?"

"It could change by tomorrow," the reservation check-in person said. "The weather here is always changeable this time of year. In a week it could be snowing."

"That's crazy," Madison said.

It was warm back home, too, where Chicagoans had enjoyed a long Indian summer. She associated regionals with colder temperatures. It seemed to Madison that many things were different about the event this year.

The check-in person was saying, "Albright. Room 517. There's continental breakfast every morning six to ten. Anything else you need call the front desk."

"Thank you," They had just pushed the elevator button when someone yelled Madison's name. Madison's skating friend, Jillian Knight, ran up and they gave each other a tight hug. Although Jillian lived in Wisconsin, the two girls competed at many of the same events. They had become fast friends over locker room chats and lunches. Once they found that they shared the same birthdate—May 26—their friendship gained a special quality. Jillian was competing in Intermediate Ladies as well.

'How are you?" Jill asked.

"Good."

"Did you just get here? I got in like an hour ago. My mom and I are going over to the rink to check in. You want to come with us?"

Madison looked at her mom for approval. "Let's put our bags down first. We'll meet you in the lobby," Mrs. Albright said.

"We'll wait right here." Jillian grinned at Madison, who smiled back. It was nice to have a friend at the competition.

Within minutes, the four met to head over to the rink. It was a five-minute car ride or fifteen-minute walk. The girls decided that it would be best for them to stretch their legs after a long day of driving so the group opted to walk. That way Jillian and Madison could catch up. It didn't take long for the subject of Caitlin's treachery to come up.

"Well," Jillian concluded in a whisper, "we have to get even this week."

"What are you thinking of doing?" Madison bit her lip. Maybe telling Jillian was a mistake. She was a big practical joker and would have no qualms about messing with Caitlin. If Caitlin's dress suddenly had a rip or her boots wound up dyed a strange color, Madison would know who was behind it.

"I have ways," Jillian smirked.

"Be careful. We don't need more drama."

"You're too nice. If a girl treated me like Caitlin treated you, I'd let her know who was boss. But I won't do anything if you don't want me to. Besides, I've had enough drama for a while too." Jillian launched into a story about how her skates had unexpectedly broken down last week. She almost had to get a new pair, but at the last minute she opted to get her skates rebuilt. Now they were usable again.

"Can you imagine trying to break in new skates in a week? That'd be almost impossible and a stupid idea. I'm so glad I didn't have to."

"Yeah, that would have been tough."

The girls approached the arena where "Welcome Regional Competitors" was emblazoned on a huge banner draped high above the entrance. The lobby was full of competitors and coaches checking in and looking at the ice surface. Madison and Jillian approached the check-in table, accepting their competitors' packet: badge, program, list of competitors, practice times, and event schedule.

The sign-in desk volunteer exclaimed, "Madison! It's great to see you. Still practicing hard, I'm sure. I bet you're skating even better."

It took Madison a moment, but she finally recognized the speaker as Rebecca, the observer who had complimented her at the Arctic Circle.

"Here's your competitor's badge and program. I'll keep an eye out for you. Good luck!"

Rebecca would have kept talking had Jillian not thanked her and dragged Madison away.

"What did she mean, 'I'll keep an eye out for you?'" Jillian demanded

"I don't know. She saw me practice back home and became kind of a fan. She's expecting me to have a great skate."

"That's a compliment. Boy, she just babbled about how great you were." A look that resembled jealousy spread across Jillian's face. "Well, whatever, let's find our moms and get out of here. I'm starving." Jillian brusquely walked away, leaving Madison standing alone feeling both embarrassed and hurt. It was not like Jillian to be jealous of anyone, let alone Madison. Nothing about this competition would be the same as ones before!

Madison still felt puzzled when Liz phoned her that night. Her coach had arrived in Minnesota a few hours before and she was calling her students to make sure that they were going to bed promptly and ready for the next day's practice.

"You don't really sound like yourself, Madison. What's going on?" Liz probed.

"That woman Rebecca from our rink talked to me today. She's telling people that I am someone to watch. That's a good thing, right?"

"Well, most people would consider that good. You, I'm not so sure about. You're not to skate great for her or anyone else. You have to do it for yourself."

"I know. I'm fine. Thanks."

"Tomorrow sleep in a little. Get a nutritious breakfast, go for a walk, and be in the lobby fifteen minutes before we have to leave for the rink."

"Got it," Madison agreed, although she didn't think she'd sleep much. As she hung up, her mother came out of the bathroom, combing damp hair.

"Was that Liz?" It struck Madison at that moment just how beautiful her mother was. She had no make-up on and her hair hung limply from her shower, but she still had an undeniable glow about her.

"Yeah. She went over when and where I'm supposed to be tomorrow. You look beautiful, mom."

Her mother laughed. "Thank you. I've still got it, I guess." She sat on the bed opposite of Madison's. "Liz is a good coach." She crawled under the covers. "You should do the same," she indicated, pointing to Madison's bed. "You need anything?"

"I'm good." Madison climbed into bed as well. "I want to sleep in a little before breakfast, though."

"All right. Night sweetheart. Love you."

"I love you too, mom."

In the dark room Madison reviewed the day's events. She was exhausted. Her less than stellar practice and the long drive had made her body ache. Jillian's jealousy was weighing heavily on Madison, too. The last thing Madison wanted was for skating to interfere with one of her closest friendships. Once Madison befriended a girl, she viewed her as a friend for life and devoted time on the friendships to keep them strong. Unfortunately, Madison had learned the hard way that other girls did not always share her view of friendship.

Madison recalled with pain how she had lost Caitlin as her best friend because of skating. Not many people knew that Caitlin and Madison were former best friends—inseparable as toddlers doing swimming, gymnastics, and ballet together. Although Caitlin's family moved several miles away when the girls were six, they remained close, seeing each other at the rink everyday. From the moment they first stepped on the ice, they both fell in love with the sport.

At first, Caitlin skated much better than Madison, but Madison improved quickly and Caitlin fell behind. Madison recalled their first skating event together, which Madison had won while Caitlin came in third. Sadly, that ended their friendship. Caitlin accused Madison of betrayal because Madison skated well and Caitlin fell twice. Caitlin left the arena huffing and had launched her mission to get back at Madison. Madison shuddered and tried to block the bad memories. She was determined not to let the same thing happen with Jillian.

Madison turned on her side and tried to sleep. What was it her mother always said? Things will look better in the morning. *Story of my life,* Madison thought as she forced herself to sleep.

10

Madison's Weighty Issue

True to her mother's words, things did look better in the morning. Madison wasn't nearly as sore and felt ready for her practice session later.

Her mom was already awake and dressed. "Jillian called. I told her you were sleeping, but she wants to have breakfast with you."

"Oh, good!" relief flooded over Madison. *Was I imagining Jillian's jealousy?* Aloud she continued, "I'll go meet her right now."

"Remember, you have to be back in the room by ten thirty to take your walk."

"I know." Madison pulled on some workout clothes and fidgeted with her hair band around a tight ponytail.

"And eat a good breakfast. A little fruit, some protein— maybe an egg or a glass of milk," her mom suggested.

Madison rolled her eyes. "I know how to eat breakfast."

Mrs. Albright sighed, "Fine. It's just you've always gone with me before so I'm there to make sure that everything is right."

"I'm a big girl. I can choose my own food."

"Yes, you can. You're growing up so fast that soon you won't need me at all."

"Mom!" Madison objected, annoyed. She ran over to her mother and gave her a hug. "I'm always gonna need you a little."

"Of course. I want you to do things on your own. Now go, or you won't have time to eat."

As Madison reached the elevator, she checked her pockets—empty. "Shoot." She raced back to her room. As she was about to knock, the door suddenly opened. "Forgetting something?" said Mrs. Albright, holding out the thin plastic card used both as the room key and meal ticket for hotel food. She was smiling. "See? I do need you," Madison laughed grabbing the key and once more kissing her mother goodbye. *Mom was right,* she thought, *at this rate, I hardly have time to eat.*

She and Jillian met in the lobby. She was dressed exceptionally well this morning. She had full make-up on— *too much,* Madison thought. Jillian's long hair hung in curls and she wore a matching pink and black tracksuit.

"You look nice," Madison said as they headed towards the buffet.

Jillian tossed her hair. "Oh, this is nothing. Besides, you never know when judges will be around. You should always look your best."

"It's not worlds, Jill," Madison teased.

"So? I'm going someday. I might as well prepare now."

"So how did you sleep?"

"Okay, but my mom snores so loudly she kept waking me up. I'll need my own room next time."

Madison just kept collecting food from the buffet. The girls took seats at a nearby table. Madison was still wondering what had gotten into Jillian. She never talked about her mom like that, and it was odd for her to be trying to impress everyone. Jillian was comfortable with herself and Madison liked that about her.

"Well, at least I'm not as sore today. What about you?" asked Madison.

"I'm fine. Geez, Maddie, are you really going to eat that?" Jillian exclaimed.

Madison paused midbite. She put her half of a whole-wheat bagel back on her plate.

"Yeah," Madison said slowly, "I was. Is that bad?"

"Well, it's not really the best food, you know."

"I'm only eating half and I'm using fat-free cream cheese, too." Madison's hand covered her bagel defensively.

Jillian voiced her disapproval, "Maddie, that's not good enough. As we get to higher levels, we really have to watch what we eat."

"I do," Madison protested. "I might have a bagel every now and then, but I eat a ton of fruit and veggies too."

"Really?" Jillian gave her a once over. "I can't really tell."

Madison looked back at Jill, wondering what she was getting at.

"I didn't want to say anything, Madison, but you look a little bigger," Jill said in a low voice.

"Yeah, I've gotten taller," Madison replied innocently.

Jillian scowled. 'No, I mean bigger this way." She spread her hands out from her sides.

"That's impossible! Liz would have said something."

"And risk your mom getting mad and maybe switching coaches? No way," Jillian countered.

"Liz is a tell-it-like-it-is coach. If something needs to be fixed, she lets me know."

"Well, she obviously let something slip through the cracks." Jillian stirred her water and waited.

Madison didn't know what to say. Jillian was way out of line. *We're friends aren't we? Why is she being so mean?*

"I'm only telling you this because you're my friend, Maddie. Friends can tell each other the truth. If we don't, who will? Just lay off food for the next few days. You'll jump better because you'll be lighter." Jillian gave her a reassuring look.

"Yeah, maybe." Madison pushed her bagel aside and started in on a piece of watermelon.

Jillian switched the conversation to school, telling Madison about her teachers and her new schedule. At ten thirty, Madison cut her off.

"I have to get back upstairs. I promised my mom."

"Okay. See you later. Do want to walk to the rink together?"

"I don't know. I'll call you." At the moment, Madison thought the answer was a definite no, but she might feel differently after her walk. Right now, she rushed back to her room, jammed the key into the door, and flung it open.

"Madison?" her mom called. Madison ignored her and went into the bathroom. She started rummaging through the cabinets.

"What are you doing?" her mom asked, leaning against the door.

"Nothing." Madison kept looking, opening cabinets and banging them closed. "Got it." She said triumphantly. She held out a scale and put in on the floor.

"What *are* you doing?" her mom demanded. Madison turned to her. "Mom, can you leave so I can do this alone?"

Her mom started to speak, but Madison cut her off. "Please? I need to do this."

Her mother turned and marched into the other room. Madison heard her slam the door that led to the balcony. Madison stripped down to her underwear and got on the scale, bracing herself for the bad news. She peered nervously at the number: 87. Exactly the same as she had been last year! Madison smiled, thinking, *I was sure I hadn't gained weight!* She stepped out of the bathroom humming and practically ran into her mother.

"So?" Mrs. Albright had her hands on her hips. 'Would you like to tell me why you ran in here looking like the sky was falling and weighed yourself?"

"I wanted to make sure I haven't gained any weight."

"And?"

"I haven't."

"Well, what a relief," Mrs. Albright said sarcastically. "Why did you need to do that?"

"People said I looked bigger."

"*Bigger?*" Mrs. Albright repeated.

"You, know, this way." She demonstrated the same gesture Jillian had used.

"Why would someone say that out of the clear blue?"

Madison shrugged. "It's no big deal. I didn't gain any weight. They were wrong."

"And if you *had* gained? What would you have done?"

Madison shifted from side to side. "I don't know. Probably I would have tried to eat less today and the rest of the week. She said that would work."

"Who's she?"

"No one, mom. Let's go for that walk." She headed for the door.

"Madison Albright, you stop right there. We are going to talk about this now."

Mrs. Albright's stopped her daughter in her tracks. "Sit," she ordered.

Madison sat. She knew better than to argue with her mother in this mood. Mrs. Albright joined Madison on the bed.

"Look. You are getting older. Someday your weight could be an issue—not because you have a problem, but because your body's going to change. It's important for you to get the right nutrition and establish good eating habits now so that the change won't be drastic."

"Will I get too fat to skate?"

"No, but your body will change. Talking about not eating these few days worries me. That could have been very dangerous, Madison. You would have become weak and you could have gotten hurt on or off the ice."

"A few days wouldn't kill me."

"No, but a few days could turn into a few weeks, a few months, or even a few years. If you want to avoid weight issues in the future, don't play with your body's needs now. If you starve yourself now, it will be harder to lose weight in the future—*if* you need to. Trust me. You only have one body. Promise me you will not play around with it."

"Mom, I think you are overreacting. I'm not gaining weight. No need to starve myself here."

"But the fact that you thought about it could mean that you might undereat in the future, and I don't want that to happen."

"Fine. Can we go for the walk now?"

"Yes. But you didn't eat breakfast. Would you like something to eat?"

"Yeah," Madison chuckled, "I'm starving. I probably wouldn't be very good at not eating."

"Let's keep it that way."

After a quick snack, Madison and her mother headed out on their walk. A trail surrounded by fall-colored trees wound from their hotel to the lake on the grounds. The pair walked in silence, each lost in her own thoughts. Madison was glad that her mother had not pressed her to reveal who had criticized her weight, thinking *I didn't want to rat Jillian out. She must be going through a difficult time. I'd rather find out what's going on and help her than turn against her.*

Madison and her mother took almost an hour to stroll around the three-mile lakefront. They returned just in time for Madison to change and head to the rink. The thought of it made her stomach do flip-flops. She wondered how many onlookers she'd have. Would Rebecca watch especially for her? Madison also hoped neither Caitlin nor Jillian would skate practice ice with her.

Once her tracksuit was zipped and her skates in their bag, she secured her hair in another tight ponytail, held with extra hairspray. To light make-up, she added a touch of mascara and lip gloss. She surveyed herself in the mirror. *Good,* she thought. Madison would put on more make-up to skate the short tomorrow, but what she wore was enough today.

On the elevator Madison psyched herself up for practice. She visualized the ice rink and how her program should be laid out. She might be first during practice to have her program music played and she wanted to be prepared.

To her surprise, Madison found Jillian waiting for her by the hotel entrance. "I thought you might not come. Let's go," Jillian said as she joined her mother in their car. "Where were you, anyway?"

"Taking a walk."

Madison and her mother drove the short route to the rink, and both girls walked into the arena. The building was abuzz with busy skaters, parents, coaches, and officials. Some parents and children were arguing. Some coaches and parents were, too. A few skaters were crying, but most looked happy and ready to go.

Madison put her skates down and began her warm-up as she scanned the crowd for a familiar face. Jillian had gone off in search of her coach and left Madison alone to prepare. Finally, she spotted Liz just as Liz spotted her, waved, and made her way over.

"Hey! How are you today?" Liz asked brightly.

"Good," replied Madison thinking, *She's in a good mood.*

"You're practice starts in thirty-five minutes. Be at the door with your skates on ten minutes before that."

"Got it. I want to get on the ice," Madison said decisively.

"Great. I'll see you in half an hour. I have to go find Caitlin and Alyssa. They're on your practice ice, too."

Madison's heart sank. She would just have to get through it. Thirty minutes couldn't be so bad, could it? Madison finished her warm-up and changed into her practice outfit—a solid navy blue dress with embroidered gold flowers and an elegant high collar. It was one of Madison's favorites, although it was not as lucky as her pink practice dress.

Ten minutes before practice, Madison stood by the boards ready to go. The Zamboni was halfway through making ice. Madison swung her arms and did deep-knee bends trying to keep warm and limber. Soon other competitors gathered by the gate to the ice. They were all Madison's age. There were some faces she recognized, but many she did not. She smiled at a few and to Madison's pleasure, they smiled back. Jillian came up decked out in an elaborate costume. It was tie-dyed blue and white with dozens and dozens of crystals outlining a diamond design in front. Madison had just enough time to nod and smile at Jillian before the gate was opened and the announcer called all of the girls' names. There was a whoosh as fourteen girls took to the ice and began stroking powerfully. The announcer read off the order for playing program music. Madison would be third to run her short on this session. Liz only called her over once during warm-up to remind her to relax her face muscles.

It seemed like just seconds before Madison's turn. She took her starting position and looked around. Her mother was in the stands. Liz and Caitlin had stopped to watch her. Jillian had stopped, too. Just as the music started, she saw Rebecca Boyle sitting nearby, whispering to someone.

Okay Madison, you can do this. Think about what you need to do, Madison ordered herself firmly.

The first few strands of "A Time for Us" from *Romeo and Juliet* blared through the rink as Madison began to move.

The eyes of many skaters, coaches, and parents followed her as she entered her first jump. Solid! A few people clapped and Madison began to relax. She skated through the rest of her short flawlessly; the whole rink echoed with applause. Madison sighed with relief and looked at the bleachers for her mom. Mrs. Albright was standing, clapping the loudest, and beaming at Madison. Madison released her ending pose and skated laps to cool down. She kept her head up, proud of this performance. It was only practice, but Madison was glad that she hadn't screwed it up under the appraising eyes of other skaters, coaches, and families. As she passed she smiled at Jillian, who just stared back blankly. Caitlin, unsurprisingly, glared her displeasure at Madison.

"Nice going," Liz approved. "I told you not to worry about yesterday. You just needed to get the kinks out. Just do your job tomorrow like today. I'm working with Melanie now. Review your spins, then footwork, in the fifteen minutes left." Liz skated away.

Madison headed into the spin circle. Her spin elements were exceptionally fast and centered dead on. She looked down at her tracings, proud that hers were the only spins that remained centered throughout. As their music played, other skaters ran through their programs, but Madison was too busy working on her own to watch. Observing other skaters made her nervous. The last to skate was Jillian. Her music, a rock n' roll/blues number, was high energy and sassy, just like Jillian. Madison caught a few elements out of the corner of her eye. Jillian missed her combination jump and stepped out of her double axel. She seemed to lose her balance on her ending spin as well. As soon as Jillian finished her disastrous short program, the Zamboni took the ice and the skaters stepped off. The locker room was quiet until Jillian banged the door as she stomped in.

"Can you believe how awful that was?" Jillian wailed, throwing herself onto the bench. She slumped against the lockers.

"It wasn't that bad," Madison offered.

"Were you watching the same program as everyone else?" shrieked Jillian. She looked around the locker room. "Wasn't it terrible?" She pointed to a redheaded skater. "You saw it. It was awful, right? Totally embarrassing."

The redhead blushed, making her red hair even more vivid. "Um, I didn't really see...just the double axel, which wasn't that bad, you just turned out of it."

Jillian turned with a harrumph back to Madison. "See?" she said. None of the skaters in the locker room knew what to say to this outburst. They silently continued to pack up their skates and stretch. Twenty minutes later Jillian and Madison emerged to their waiting mothers and coaches. Mrs. Albright and Liz stood next to each other, smiling. Madison's mother hugged her. Jillian looked a little lost and twitchy. Mrs. Knight talked intently with Jill's coach, Dimitri, until she saw Jillian and arched her eyebrow.

"Jillian! Dimitri and I want to talk to you."

Jillian shot Madison a look, pulled herself up, and made her way to her mother and coach. None of them looked happy.

Mrs. Albright put an arm around Madison. "Come on, let's go back to the hotel. We have a lot to do before tomorrow and you have an early start time." Her mother tugged at her gently, but Madison remained still.

"Why don't we wait for Jillian?" she asked.

Mrs. Albright and Liz exchanged glances. Neither spoke. The scene unfolding was not good. Both Jillian's mother and her coach appeared to be lecturing Jillian at once and their body language showed that what they were saying wasn't nice. Jillian, shoulders slumping, looked as if she might cry. Luckily, Jillian never showed others that they were getting the best of her.

Finally, it was Liz who spoke. "Madison," she began softly, "I know Jillian is your friend, but whatever is going on over there is a matter for skater, coach, and mother. It could take some time. It's not good to have spectators eavesdropping."

Madison surveyed the situation once more. Now only Dimitri was talking, but Jillian's mother was nodding, clearly agreeing with him. Madison suddenly understood why Jillian had been acting so differently. She must be under tremendous pressure from her new coach and her mom. Something was going on that Jillian was not sharing, and Madison hoped that she would find out before the end of regionals. As she watched Jillian's shoulders slump further and further forward, Madison realized that Liz was right. This was Jillian's business and she didn't need Madison watching.

"Okay. Let's go." Madison bit her lip. She looked over her shoulder one more time at Jillian and then Madison, her mother, and Liz left the arena.

Madison was silent on the car ride back. Mrs. Albright and Liz were making small talk in the front seat, but Madison's thoughts kept returning to Jillian and her mother. Madison had never seen Mrs. Knight act so angry at the rink, and Madison had always thought that Jillian and her mother shared a good relationship, like Madison's with her own mother. It was sad to find she was wrong, and Madison wondered how long this situation had been going on.

She still thought about what could have changed for Jillian and her mother when Mrs. Albright announced, "We're back at the hotel. Everybody out."

She studied Madison for a long moment. *Seeing how upset I am*, Madison guessed, pulling out her skate bag behind her. The three walked into the lobby. It was jam packed with skaters heading to practice or just coming back.

Liz faced Madison. "I still have a few students practicing tonight, so you're on your own. I'll call later to check on you. Go for another walk, rest. Try not to obsess about tomorrow," she smiled at Madison, "and eat, please—no crazy diet changes." Liz tapped Madison's shoulder, but her voice was not angry.

"Mom!" Madison shot her mother a horrified stare. She didn't want Liz to know everything she did, especially about her fitness to skate.

"No, Madison," Liz said firmly. "I'm glad your mother mentioned it. We won't make a big deal about it. Just don't start doing anything stupid. A skater who becomes too weak from undereating to jump or spin is no good to anyone."

Madison hung her head: *Liz is right. How could I even think about jeopardizing my health?*

"I won't do it again. Besides, I get too hungry when I don't eat," Madison joked. Then she became serious. "Do you think Jillian is trying to starve herself?"

Liz's expression was hard to read. "I don't know. It's not something you should ask anyone else. That would be a terrible rumor to start. If you suspect that, you can ask her about it *after* the competition. It looks like Jillian has enough to deal with already." Liz checked her watch. "I've got to run. See you later. Good job today!"

Liz dashed out to the waiting shuttle bus that took coaches and officials to the rink.

After stowing the skating bags in their room, Madison and her mother came out into the open air. The weather had really been cooperating, although it was a little cooler today. They walked around the lake again. The multicolored trees seemed more vibrant than they had been hours earlier.

Madison grew tense as she walked. Her thoughts about Jillian in the back of her mind, she thought too about what tomorrow's performance meant for her skating career. The butterflies took flight again in her stomach and she noted, *They feel more like slugs than butterflies!* Butterflies made her want to go out and skate; slugs made her want to dive into bed and hide under the covers. Madison swallowed, hoping to make the slugs disappear. She tried again and again as they approached the hotel. No luck. She felt too nauseous to eat. *Great,* she thought, *now mom and Liz will think that I don't want to eat because I think I'm too fat!* Madison rolled her eyes and harrumphed.

"Honey, you're awfully quiet. Are you okay?" Mrs. Albright asked.

"I'm fine." She really wasn't in the mood to talk about everything.

"A lot has been going on lately," her mother continued, "so it would make sense if you were a little more nervous than usual before competing."

Madison shrugged, "I'm not. I skated fine today. You saw—everybody clapped."

"I know and that's great, but I'm just saying it's all right to admit being more tense."

The two stood in front of the elevator. Madison jabbed the up button fiercely.

"Why do you keep saying that I'm so nervous?" she asked angrily, pushing the level five button so hard that her mother had to remove her hand to stop her from breaking it.

"Calm down. I'm trying to help. Don't make it a big deal. If you want to talk, we will. If not, we don't have to. Whatever helps you get ready for tomorrow," Mrs. Albright said gently. She swung open the door to their room.

"I'm *fine,* mom. I'm upset with how Jill's been acting, and Caitlin has been hard to take lately, but I'm a tough competitor, remember? You and Liz say that you never have to worry about me."

"But that doesn't mean that we expect you to be strong all the time."

"Mom! I am fine! Please, just let's not talk about this, okay?" Madison bellowed. She surprised even herself. She had never raised her voice to her mother before. Mrs. Albright was taken aback as well. Madison quickly changed her tone.

"Sorry, mom. Maybe I am nervous. But talking about it will only make it worse…right?" she asked.

"Not always the best way to handle it. I can't force you, but if you decide to talk, I'm here."

Madison smiled. "Thanks." She flopped on the bed and took out a magazine she had brought from home. Now was the perfect time for both of them to focus on something else.

"I think I'll go call your dad." With that, Mrs. Albright left the room. Madison sighed heavily. The magazine distraction wasn't working. She could really use something else to think about. She searched the room looking for a good book or the remote for the TV. She was checking the front pocket of her duffle bag when her cell phone rang.

"Hello?"

"Oh my gosh, you've got to help me!" Jordan's voice wailed.

"Jordan, what's wrong?" She was used to calming down Jordan, who could be overly dramatic.

"My life is over! Jackie asked Tyler to the Halloween fair today!"

"But he asked you and you said you would go. What's the problem?"

"The problem? The problem is he said yes!" Jordan sobbed. Madison was definitely distracted now.

"Why? Did he say why?"

"Because she is so popular. You know—one of Caitlin's friends. He says he likes me better and maybe we could go somewhere else, some other time." Her voice turned bitter. "But I don't want to go anywhere with him, ever."

"You shouldn't. He's an idiot. You should tell him off." Madison was not good at confronting people, but she knew Jordan could put people in their place.

"What would I say? 'You have to go to the fair with me?' Yeah, that'll work," Jordan responded sarcastically.

"I don't know, but you should say something. Don't just accept it. You're good at things like this. Say what you feel."

There was silence on the other end as Jordan pondered what Madison had said. After a pause, Jordan decided, "Okay. I will talk to him tomorrow. I will tell him exactly what I feel." Madison could hear her flicking her bracelets. She imagined Jordan getting right in Tyler's face and setting him straight. A second later, Jordan was changing topics.

"So, what's up with you? How's the competition?"

"I had a good practice today. Now I'm just relaxing and getting ready for tomorrow. I have to get up at six. I compete at seven thirty."

"Wow. I won't even be at school yet and you'll be done already. Then you can go back to sleep if you want," Jordan said enviously.

"Yeah," Madison heard the key turning in the lock. "Hey, my mom just got back. I have to go. Let me know how things work out. Call me if you need me."

They finished their goodbyes just as Mrs. Albright came in.

"You ready to get a snack and walk around some more?" she asked Madison.

"Yeah." Madison replied, and they headed out the door. She was glad to leave the hotel room, where all she could concentrate on were the skates and costumes that stared back at her.

11

The Long Short Program

Her less-than-peaceful night began with Madison visualizing herself falling on one jump after another, but after what seemed like hours, she could visualize herself landing each jump. *Man, I hope this goes well! Please let me skate well,* were the last thoughts she remembered before sleep claimed her.

The phone rang with her wake-up call. A groggy Madison felt like she had just fallen asleep. But the instant Madison sat up, she felt a surge of excitement and anticipation. She just hoped the good butterflies would last. As her mom strode around their room, Madison took stock. Unfortunately, the butterflies in her stomach were being devoured by the slugs. The jubilation of being able to perform was disappearing, replaced by the fear of going out there and, well, blowing it.

"Morning sunshine," Mrs. Albright said. "The bathroom is all yours. Hurry up and get ready so we can grab breakfast before you go." Mrs. Albright was always cheery in the morning, a trait that Madison had only partly inherited—when she was doing something she loved, like skating alone to music that echoed inside.

After a quick shower and tooth brushing, Madison dressed in her warm-up clothes. Her mom usually applied her make-up for competitions. Madison swirled on foundation and blush, but it was Mrs. Albright's job to highlight Madison's eyes to look big and beautiful. Madison's eye make-up accented their unusual, light honey brown color. The warm hues of eye shadow her mom was using made the eyes pop. As Mrs. Albright painted on the different shades and added liner and mascara, Madison tried to calm down. She didn't say much, but Mrs. Albright was used to that. Madison became eerily quiet the day of an event, thereby giving nothing of her growing tension away.

"Done." Her mother pushed her toward the mirror. "What do you think?"

Madison looked hard at herself. Her mom had done a great job. She looked beautiful—especially for six o'clock in the morning. Despite the frantic moments of, where are the car keys and do we have the music, fifteen minutes later the two finally descended to the lobby. There was a tense atmosphere in the hotel lobby. Lots of skaters—the girls adorned with glittery hair in tight buns and the boys in sleek competition costumes that made them look tall, slim, and older—stood around looking nervous, making last-minute costume checks.

Madison followed her mom to the continental breakfast buffet.

"What do you want to eat?" Mrs. Albright asked.

"Oh, um, nothing. I'm not really hungry."

"Madison!"

"Not because of *that*," She said, annoyed. "I get too nervous to eat before I skate."

"A little something won't hurt. How 'bout a yogurt or a piece of fruit? Toast is always good."

Madison looked over the selection. "I'll take some toast and orange juice, I guess." She grabbed a napkin and slid the whole-wheat bread in the toaster.

Madison and Mrs. Albright headed for the door just as Jillian emerged from the elevator. "Jill! Jillian, hi!" Madison waved. Jillian saw Madison. Instead of returning the greeting, Jillian turned her back and stormed off to the buffet. Her mother was right behind her. Madison froze, stunned that Jillian had just blown her off. Jillian looked over the buffet before finally settling on a few slices of fruit—definitely not the right fuel on a competition day. She showed the fruit to her mother, who nodded approval. It dawned on Madison that Jillian might not be dieting by choice.

"Come on, you're going to be late," Mrs. Albright urged.

Madison followed in silence. The skater's initial shock had turned to anger, then curiosity, and finally worry for her friend. But now was not the time to worry about Jillian. Madison's event was in an hour, and last night's images of a bad skate had not vanished.

Before Madison knew it, the car stopped at the rink's entrance. Her mom gave Madison a reassuring smile. Madison blew her a kiss and followed the throng of skaters and coaches inside. To her dismay, she saw Rebecca sitting at the music drop-off table. Madison frantically looked around to find another registration table, but Rebecca had spotted her before Madison could budge.

"Madison, hi. So today's the day!" Rebecca smiled.

"Yes, in about an hour." Madison replied dully.

"Well, I'll be watching. The word's out with everyone who is working the show: you're one of the skaters to watch. We're excited to see your performance. I know you're going to make us proud." Rebecca stated confidently.

"I hope so," Madison responded. Her name checked off and music checked in, Madison hurried to the dressing room, trying to convince herself, *A few extra people watching is a good thing. They think I have talent and could go somewhere in this sport. I should feel important, and the extra people cheering might give me an edge over the competitors.* Madison started to warm up, as she did every morning. Only this morning each movement felt heavier and harder to do. The warm-up that had been so routine was now a struggle. *I've gotta shake this off,* she thought with alarm. She was doing floor jumps beside the boards when Liz came by.

With a small hug, Liz asked, "How are you today?"

"I feel nervous, actually." Madison admitted and relaxed some. Perhaps it had been a mistake not to express how troubled she felt.

"Nervous about what?" Liz demanded impatiently. Madison pictured Liz as one of those skaters who just went out and repeated flawlessly what she'd done in practice—no stress, no unbelievable case of nerves. Madison didn't think Liz would understand.

71

"We all get nervous. Heck, even I get a bit nervous for my skaters from time to time. But it depends on what you do with those nerves. Do you control them or do you let them control you?" Liz replied in a slightly more gentle tone.

"I don't know why I'm jittery. I just am." This wasn't completely true. Madison could list plenty of reasons why she was anxious, but Liz did not seem ready to understand them.

"Well, a few jitters are good. You need to learn how to work with them. Let me see you walk through your program." Liz said, changing the subject. Clearly, there was no room for frayed nerves this morning, and Madison hoped that she would regain control of her emotions in the next thirty minutes.

After she had run through her short twice on the floor and had successfully landed her jumps off ice, Madison entered the locker room to change. She had no need to check the list for other skaters in her group; she would see who was preparing in the locker room. Sure enough, both Jillian and Caitlin were sliding into their costumes. Madison had vainly hoped that neither skater would be competing directly against her, but instead she was forced to skate against both. Madison sat down, noticing that Jillian had put her things directly next to hers.

"Hey, Jillian." Madison said tentatively. Jillian continued to wrap her long dark hair up into a bun. Silence.

Madison sighed and was determined to get a word out of Jillian before their five-minute warm-up.

"How was the rest of your day? Mine was good. We walked around the lake and then the town."

"As if I would care what the champion skater does with her free time," Jillian cut her off.

Madison was shocked into temporary silence. "What are you talking about?" she asked in bewilderment.

Jillian shrugged. "You know," was her only response.

"No, I don't know." Madison said as anger surged through her. "Jill, you've been acting really weird this week. What's up?"

"Nothing. I'm just tired of you trying to upstage me."

Madison had no idea what Jillian meant. She was only trying to be Jill's good friend. There was no time to respond, however. It was time to wait rinkside for the five-minute warm-up.

Instead, Madison simply said, "Good luck, Jill."

Jillian stiffened slightly but didn't wish Madison good luck in turn. A wave of hurt washed over Madison as she adjusted her beautiful pink and white tie-dyed dress and laced up her skates. She desperately blocked the dispute out of her mind as she raced to the boards. The Zamboni was just finishing the ice.

"Where have you been?" Liz glared at her and hissed, "You were supposed to be here ten minutes ago."

"Sorry. I had trouble with my dress," Madison lied. The judges and technical panelists filed in to take their seats behind devices that would record their scores. Parents and spectators settled into the stands.

Suddenly there was a loud crackle as the announcer's voice came over the sound system. "Will the next group of skaters please take the ice? This will be Intermediate Ladies Group B, first warm-up. Alyssa Carlton, Erica Mallory, Caitlin Jackson, Madison Albright, and Jillian Knight." The announcer's voice silenced and background music filled the arena as the competitors shot out of the gate with a bang, each trying to prove she was the fastest, the best skater. Madison stroked among them but easily made her way to the head of the pack as she completed forward and then backward crossovers. No need to look at Liz; Madison had her warm-up down.

After she completed her spins, Liz called her over. "Next warm up your jumps."

Madison skated away just as Caitlin glided toward Liz. The two held each other's gaze until Caitlin sneered at Madison, who decided, *Let it go.* If she barely had time to worry about a problem with her good friend Jillian, she certainly wasn't going to let Caitlin's snub interfere with her warm-up. Despite her apprehensiveness, her warm-up was solid. *See,* she told herself. *You're fine.* A split second later the announcer gave a one-minute warning. Madison saw Alyssa skate over to the boards. She was the first to compete and needed time now to clear her head and shed her jacket. Madison quickly ran through her footwork and finished just as the announcer called time.

The remaining skaters cleared the ice and Alyssa stood alone. It was awful to be the first skater in the group and Madison was grateful not to be. Madison slipped on her skateguards, walked away from the ice, and leaned against the arch that led to the locker room. This was the horrible part: the waiting. At such moments nerves would either consume the skater and she would fall apart, or the competitor would pull herself together and skate a great program. Jillian sat on a bench, head down, staring at the floor in deep concentration. Erica did deep knee bends. Caitlin paced up and down the hallway. Madison usually tried to stand completely alone and focus on herself. There was no such spot this morning. Instead, Madison listened to the crowd's response to Alyssa. They clapped. Alyssa must have landed one of her jumps. Then the crowd gasped, and seconds later, gasped again. Clearly, Alyssa was not having a great skate. Her music finished and the crowd applauded politely.

When Alyssa appeared backstage, her coach had her arm around the red-faced skater; she was weeping softly. Madison reached out and touched her arm in consolation. Madison heard only one gasp from the audience, so she assumed that the next competitor had put on a decent performance.

"Keep yourself warm. Don't just stand there. You're not watching everyone, are you?" Liz frowned.

"No." Madison said quickly.

"Good. Caitlin is next and then I will come for you, okay?"

"Okay."

Liz had a point. From an early age, she had been taught not to watch the skaters competing before her. She shouldn't have been listening to the crowd's reaction to their skating, either. Madison started mimicking her jumps off ice. Her arms felt both heavy and limp. Her head felt fuzzy, too. The whole scene was swirling before her and suddenly she couldn't see clearly. The butterflies were banging against her sides, trying fiercely to escape. Madison bent down and shook her head. Her competition anxiety was ten times worse today. *Why?* she thought in panic. *I skated a great warm-up. Everyone's rooting for me. They expect me to skate great—really, they*

expect me to win this event. I see it written all over their faces.
Madison stood slowly but couldn't shake these feelings off.
Applause for Caitlin's program ended; it was now her turn
to skate. She had already taken off her warm-up sweater but
shook as though freezing. The rest of her body felt as limp as
her arms.

She stepped onto the ice as Caitlin got off. Caitlin said
nothing, which was both a surprise and a relief. Liz stood right
there to hug Caitlin, which explained Caitlin's silence.

"Good luck." Caitlin gave Madison a syrupy smile.

Liz took her hands. "Go out and do what you know how to
do. Think of the words I told you as you go into each element—
no more, no less. And breathe. You can do it!" Liz squeezed her
hands and smiled. Madison smiled back weakly.

"Let's give a warm welcome to Madison Albright,
representing the Arctic Circle Figure Skating Club," the
announcer's voice boomed.

Madison stroked out, presented herself, and settled into her
starting position. She avoided looking into the audience, afraid
of seeing the expectant eyes looming at her. And she especially
didn't want to catch the eye of anyone she knew. Her arms still
felt heavy in their sockets and she was praying that no one saw
her legs trembling. She fleetingly wondered how Caitlin skated
before the music shook her back to reality.

Hearing the familiar music was comforting and Madison
began to move with more ease. Her layback spin was fast
as always and greeted with applause. Not many people got
applause for their spins, so Madison knew hers must have
been exceptional.

Next, the double axel. *Breathe,* Madison told herself,
*gather speed, think lift, and then you'll fall—er, land—like
you always have.* Panic struck. *Why think of falling at a
time like this?* It was too late to center her thoughts. Her
last thought was, *Don't fall!* as she took off. The jump was a
blur and before she knew it, she hit the ice hard. The crowd
groaned. She immediately pictured the disappointment on
her mom's and Liz's faces and the smug expression on
Caitlin's. Madison wanted to disappear on the spot, but
she had to keep going. Madison hurried to her feet and

kept moving. Her body did as it was told but her mind was somewhere completely different.

She tried to forget the fall as she prepared for her triple toe. She went into this jump thinking, *Please let me land this!* The landing was shaky, with a slight turn out of the jump. *Deduction again,* Madison thought woefully. She went into her spiral sequence, ignoring the music. At this point she was just trying to finish the program without any further disasters. She managed a small smile at the judges as she glided past in a perfectly arched and split spiral.

Only one more hurdle remained: her double flip-double loop combination. She took a deep breath and for the first time managed to think about technique instead of blindly hoping that she would land her jumps. Madison landed her double flip—not perfectly—and had to throw herself into the double loop to get off the ice. Somehow, she pulled it off. She headed into her footwork sequence. *Almost done. Come on, stay focused,* Madison coached herself. The first half was fine. Crossing the center line, she lost her footing and had to put a hand on the ice to keep from falling. *Come on, really?* Madison was furious with herself for letting this happen. She went into her final combination spin, which ironically rotated faster than ever. She tended to wind herself up harder when she was mad, making her spin like a top. She struck her final pose. The audience clapped.

Madison was too frightened to dare look up. She bowed to each side and skated off. Liz stood at the gate, looking puzzled. Madison fell into her outstretched arms. It was not like the hug she would have gotten had she skated well. They moved away as Jillian stepped onto the ice for her short. Liz put her hands on Madison's shoulders, looked her in the eye, and asked sharply "What happened out there?"

The skater's held-back tears now spilled over like a fountain. Liz let her sob for a moment, but then said, "Madison stop crying. It's not good for people to see."

Madison rubbed her eyes and swallowed a few sobs to collect herself. She was still sniffling and her voice quivering as she asked, "Liz, what does this mean? Will I not make final round? What if I don't get out of the region? I'll never make my goal." Madison bit her lip to stop the tears threatening to leak out once more.

"Well, the results aren't posted yet. Even with these few mistakes, you should be okay. Other girls made a lot more. Your program wasn't bad. But making final round is not concerning me. What happened to make you skate down from your usual performance?"

*Well let's see. Caitlin trying to screw me up, Jillian acting strange, Rebecca telling everyone to watch me, the announcement at school, everyone expecting me to win, not wanting to disappoint you or my mom, the dog I can't get if I don't skate well....*Madison's mental list went on and on, unspoken.

"I don't know. I couldn't control my nerves." Madison's eyes blurred with tears as she stared down at her skates. She was sure that Liz was furious with her.

"You need a better explanation than that. When I used to get nervous, I was competing at nationals or worlds. This is just regionals."

Liz didn't understand. Any explanation, Madison felt, would fall on deaf ears.

"Look, just because I never got real nervous doesn't mean that all my students will react like me. We'll wait for the results, then talk about what to do. It'll work out," the coach reassured her.

Those last few words were too little too late from Liz. "It'll work out" was a feeble attempt at an apology. Madison was not prepared to accept it. Reassurance from Liz didn't happen. The announcer introduced the next Intermediate group. She had half an hour to wait to learn whether she had made the top six and qualified for the final round. Madison sat on the locker room bench to remove her skates.

Looking up, she found Caitlin looming over her. "I saw you fall. Tragic."

"And how did you skate, Caitlin?" Madison asked as she looked over to see Jillian, standing hands on her hips looking menacingly at Caitlin.

Jillian wiggled her finger at Caitlin. "Didn't you fall twice and step out of a spin?" she asked. "Or was that someone else?"

Pure hatred twisted Caitlin's lips. "You must be mistaken." Her tone was breezy, but she quickly gathered her bag and marched out of the locker room looking humiliated.

Madison turned to Jillian. "Thanks."

"Don't mention it. She had it coming." The last of the other skaters left the locker room. Jillian rocked back and forth on her heels before she rushed over to Madison and gave her a hug.

"I'm so sorry, Madison!" she cried. "I didn't want to be mean to you. When I heard you messed up today I knew that my being mean to you was a reason for it."

"No, no of course it wasn't," Madison lied.

"Can I just explain myself, please?" When Madison nodded in encouragement, Jillian uneasily continued. "It's been really hard lately. My new coach Dimitri says mean things about my skating. He and my mom think that will make me better. He criticizes everything about me! My mom says some coaches are that way and that's why their students win. She isn't much better. Money's been pretty tight, and she says she wants to make sure that she's getting results. She threatened to make me stop skating if I don't make it to the final round. And threatened to stop skating lessons if I didn't win."

Madison forgot about her own performance. Jillian went on, "But none of this should have made me mean to you. Only they kept comparing me to you. They said your body is better than mine, your costumes are prettier, and you even look better than I do on the ice. Yesterday, they kept comparing my practice with how great you skated and said I couldn't hold a candle to you. The pressure is wearing me out. I have no idea if I'm a good skater anymore! I don't know a good practice from a bad one; when I'm trying hard or not. And I was so jealous of you. How well you skate, how nice your mom is—she's so supportive! She could care less if you come in dead last as long as you're happy."

"I know. But I have my pressures, too. And they got the better of me today."

"I wish I had your pressure. You just worry about doing what everyone thinks you're going to. You only have to worry about beating yourself. I have to worry about even staying in the game." Jillian was wistful.

"Jill, that's not true. You need to fix your situation—it's not healthy. Why can't you talk to your mom?"

"Because she only cares about winning and skating as well as she *thinks* I should. She doesn't believe me when I tell her that she is hurting my feelings. She just thinks I'm overly sensitive."

"Well, it doesn't sound like it to me."

There was a knock on the door. "Madison, are you in there? Are you okay, honey?" Mrs. Albright opened the door. Her mother rushed her and gave her a big hug.

"You did fine, Maddie. Don't worry about a few mistakes; you can do better tomorrow. Are you upset?" Mrs. Albright looked over Madison's expression and pulled her into another hug. "You are upset. It's okay. We'll talk about it when we get home. Do you want to watch the rest of the Intermediate groups?"

"Yeah. Can Jill come with us?"

Mrs. Albright seemed to notice Jillian for the first time. "Of course. Come on. Jill. You did a nice job today."

"Thanks, Mrs. Albright." Jillian looked relieved that someone didn't criticize her skating.

They watched the last Intermediate Ladies group warm up. Madison had to be in the top six out of twelve from her classification to make the final round.

At last, the last skater stepped off to applause and the Zamboni emerged to clean the ice. Madison stayed put. More than waiting to go on the ice, she dreaded waiting for the results. Jillian tapped her shoulder.

"The zam is almost done. We should probably check the results." Jillian had reason to be nervous, too. The results sheet would be posted on an office window. Mrs. Albright looked at Madison, silently asking whether to accompany her to view the sheet. Today it was torture enough with just Jillian along. The posting was easy to spot. A crowd of anxious skaters gathered in front of a window pushing to peer at the results. Madison stopped about three feet from the window. Jillian asked, "Aren't you coming?"

"I can't. I don't want to know."

Jillian stomped her foot. "You *have* to look. If you have to skate tomorrow, you need to be ready." Jillian grabbed her hand, practically dragging her. "I don't know what you're so worried about. I'm sure you made it to the next round. Even with a few mistakes you did better than most of the competitors."

Madison would not believe that until she saw the results. Madison approached the window reluctantly. Studying some of the skaters' reactions, she could tell where each had placed just by her face. Madison tried to count the happy faces to see if the qualifying spots had been taken, but lost track.

"Harrumph! Come on," Jillian ordered. She scrolled down the list with her index finger.

"Ha," she said triumphantly. "I got fourth."

Madison was standing next to Jillian with her hand over her eyes. "Great!" What did I get?"

"Look for yourself."

Madison slowly lowered her hand and looked at the posting. Third.

"I can't believe it. Even with my mistakes?" she asked in wonderment.

Jillian punched her lightly on the arm. "Well, yeah! I mean, why were you worried? Sure jumps carry more weight in this judging system, but they aren't everything. Your spins and footwork were the highest level of anyone's."

Madison double-checked the results. She had seen correctly; she'd made it to final round. If she skated well tomorrow, she could still accomplish her goal. Frustrated, Madison thought, *I don't deserve to be third, I made more than one error. Why did they place me that high?*

Jillian's stare startled Madison out of her thoughts. "What is your problem? We both made it through. Aren't you happy?" Jillian pouted as if to say, you'd better at least be happy for me.

"Yes, Jill. Let's go tell everyone the news." Her mom and Liz were talking at the arena entrance, her mother wearing a worried look.

"I got third." Madison said. She didn't fake her mom out by pretending she had placed worse.

Mrs. Albright clapped her hands. "Oh, thank God. I was so worried! You get to move on! That's great." She paused. 'Not that I would have been disappointed if you hadn't done so well."

"I know Mom. Jill got fourth. We both made it to final round."

Liz put her arms around her. "Congratulations. Your work paid off." Madison smiled weakly. No need to ask Liz why she had placed so high. When Liz was happy, you didn't rock the boat.

"Go back to the hotel now. Rest. Your next practice is at four thirty. Be here forty-five minutes early," Liz ordered.

Madison spotted Jillian receiving hugs from both her mother and her coach. Hopefully Jillian's good skating would last through tomorrow.

The whole morning was a blur. It was only nine thirty, but she had already competed, placed, and knew she would compete in the finals. Everything had happened so fast!

She wanted to be happy to make final round, to have placed third. Wouldn't anyone else be? But Madison was disappointed and confused. At the very moment she was to skate her short, Madison had forgotten everything she learned. Her mind blanked completely and her body froze. She was lucky to have skated as well as she did. This degree of nervousness was crippling to an athlete. Madison couldn't deal with these jitters, and Liz couldn't either. *The best I can do is sleep and hope they go away. I didn't totally blow it, so there's no reason to stay nervous,* Madison decided.

12

Final Round Practice

The hotel lobby looked much the same as it had earlier. Skaters rushed around preparing for their event, coaches and parents were lounging on the couches. Madison skirted the whole scene to get to her room. She buried her head in the pillow and cried. She wasn't even sure why, but she couldn't stop the tears from spilling over. Madison heard the key turn in the lock. She tried desperately to reach the bathroom before her mother stepped in and saw Madison stuck halfway between the bedroom and bathroom door.

"I thought so," Mrs. Albright said. "I knew something was wrong."

"Mom, it's fine," Madison protested.

"I don't think so. I can tell by your face. Besides, you've been crying."

"How do you know that? Why do you always push me to tell you stuff?"

"Madison, I am not pushing for anything," Mrs. Albright said sternly. "But this is not like asking what you got on an algebra test or what boy you like. This is a much bigger deal."

"I don't want to talk about it!" Madison shouted and slammed the bathroom door shut.

Mrs. Albright waited patiently before tapping on the door. "You know you're going to have to come out of there pretty soon. You're hungry and your food is out here."

Eventually, Madison quietly opened the door. "Sorry," she mumbled, taking her snack from Mrs. Albright's hand.

Madison ate in silence and avoided eye contact with her mom. Finally, Madison couldn't take the silence anymore and broke down. *But only to a point,* she reminded herself. *Don't tell her everything.*

"I'm disappointed with how I skated, okay? I wish I had done better."

"Well, honey, we always wish that we could have done something better. But do you think that that was the best you could skate at that moment?"

"No," Madison denied. "No, I could have done so much better. You saw the warm-up. I just froze out there once they called my name."

"I wouldn't say you froze—"Mrs. Albright started, but Madison cut her off,

"No, I did. I could have done everything perfectly and I didn't." The tears were welling up again. "And I don't think I deserved third."

Mrs. Albright cupped Madison's chin in her hand. "Look. I watched every single girl out there today. They all made mistakes, including you. But you had something extra. I don't know what it is, but all your elements look better. More polished. Liz said your levels were high enough on your spins and spirals and all that to put you third."

"But I didn't earn it."

"You are the only one who thinks that. You can feel sorry for yourself or you can prepare for tomorrow. Tomorrow is a new day, a new program."

Madison knew her mom was trying to help. She had—a little. But the ache in her stomach remained. "Can I take a nap now?" she asked.

"Yes. We'll take a walk later."

Under the covers Madison repeated her mom's words. She was right. Madison could turn this attitude around. She didn't *have* to be nervous; it was her choice. Madison spent the next ten minutes trying to picture herself as a strong, confident girl in control of her emotions. It went well until the image of her falling reappeared and refused to go away.

***

"Madison, hurry up! You're late," Liz called as Madison hurried to the gate. She was only five minutes late for her practice, but Liz was not pleased. "That's no way to show me your focus," she snapped. Madison groaned inwardly. Just this once she really wanted to tell Liz to shut it, but she knew she couldn't. There was no faster way to get on the bad side of a coach than to disrespect her—especially at competition in front of skaters and parents.

"Madison, Madison, are you with it?" Liz snapped her fingers in front of Madison's face.

Madison grimaced. "Yes, Liz. I just got here. Can you please give me a minute to settle in?" Madison tried to be polite.

"I suppose so. I'll go find Alyssa. She made it to final round, too. Just start warming up." Liz said. She gave a curt nod and disappeared.

Madison stomped the floor. *Why was Liz so uptight at competition? Sure, it was stressful; she wanted all of her students to do well, but was it necessary to snap at everyone? Especially me,* Madison thought angrily, *I'm already upset and I'm not doing anything wrong. My mom isn't even a problem....*

In this practice, she would see the final round competitors. Madison stretched and looked at the other skaters. Caitlin wasn't among the finalists, Madison realized smugly. Jordan was right: even if she didn't skate her best, Madison had skated better than Caitlin.

Madison spotted a clock. Her stomach lurched; ten minutes to icetime. She threw on her violet practice dress and dashed to the ice. She slowed down as she filed in line with the other girls. She couldn't spot Liz anywhere. *Whew,* Madison thought, *I really dodged a bullet there.*

"Will the next group of skaters take the ice for practice?" the announcer called. Madison could feel the energy shift throughout the pack of girls taking the ice. Everyone wanted to skate her best this practice. The judges and callers would be watching. Although the judges were supposed to judge the skaters on the day of the actual event, it was common knowledge that the judges picked their favorite skaters based on practice.

The announcer read the playing order for program music. Madison heard her name first. She winced. She hated going first; she was never quite warmed up enough. After five minutes the announcer came over the loud speaker, the announcer called her turn for music.

Just as Madison put her toepick in the ice for the opening pose, the music started and Madison lurched forward. *Only five seconds into the program and I'm already behind! So much for looking relaxed,* Madison grunted. Madison's long program opened with a spin. It helped her center herself, literally, and it always drew applause from the crowd. Madison executed her layback perfectly and moved onto the double flip-double loop combination. She landed it. Madison grinned and began skating with less tension.

Nothing to worry about, she told herself. She landed her double axel and executed her spiral sequence. The triple toe was up next. Liz had told her to single it and do the triple later in the session. But Madison was skating confidently. Seconds before she took off, Madison decided to try the jump. She launched herself into the air spun two-and-a-half revolutions and came down hard on the ice. Images of Liz banging the boards flashed before Madison as she stood up to continue. Liz had been right; Madison should have left out the triple toe. She set out to prove that she could recover from that mistake.

Her footwork went without a glitch and she prepared for her double Lutz-double toe combination. *Piece of cake,* Madison boasted as she took off. Bam! She fell again. Now Madison panicked. What was going on? Falling on the triple toe had thrown her slightly, but she was shocked that the rest of her program went downhill. She singled the rest of her jumps, although her spins were well done. The music ended and Madison held her position for five long seconds afterward, tears brimming under her eyelids. The audience clapped, although half-heartedly, and Madison curtsied and skated around. She kept her head down. She did not want to face Liz now, after disobeying her and skating as poorly as she had.

"Madison," Liz's voice reached her. Madison ignored her and skated another lap. "Madison!" Liz repeated, louder. Madison skated yet another lap, hoping that Liz would move onto another student and Madison could avoid her.

"Madison, come here!" Liz's voice had an edge. Madison stopped in front of Liz, still keeping her head down.

"Why did you try the triple toe? I told you to leave it out." Liz questioned sternly.

"I felt up to trying it."

"Well, look what happened. Why did you let the miss affect you so badly?"

"I kept thinking I shouldn't have done it and how mad you were going to be and that everyone saw me fall."

"Keep your focus better. I'm not as mad that you tried the triple toe as I am that you couldn't pull yourself together after you fell."

"I'm disappointed about that, too."

"I just don't know what's gotten into you this week. You're usually such a tough competitor. Why are you so nervous?"

"I don't know," Madison said dully. That was true. She didn't know why she was freezing up and why her brain shut off every time she skated.

"I have to move on. Run through all the sections again and work on your jumps. Tonight I want you to relax and visualize yourself doing the perfect program over and over."

"Okay," Madison grumbled, recalling what had been happening whenever she pictured herself skating.

Liz's expression softened. "Maddie, you are doing really well. Don't worry about pleasing everyone else or skating great for them. Just worry about yourself. Promise?"

Madison nodded. Liz winked before moving onto Melanie. During the rest of the practice, Madison would land a jump, then miss it, then land it again. This cycle continued as a slew of long programs played around her. For the first time Madison was oblivious to the other skaters and their music, determined to turn her practice into a good one. But each time she did a move correctly, she did two incorrectly. Finally, after an agonizing thirty minutes, the practice session ended. She cooled down and took her skates off with lightening speed.

She found her mother in the lobby. "Let's get out of here," Madison ordered and shot out the door. Mrs. Albright followed close on her heels.

"Madison, what's the matter?"

Madison didn't reply. She was already in the car, buckling her seat belt. Mrs. Albright threw her a sideways glance as she backed the car out of the parking space. Madison had waited long enough; she burst into tears.

13

The Final Score

Madison lay awake Friday night thinking thousands of thoughts. Was Jordan sitting at home? Probably not. Jordan would show up following a personal catastrophe, smiling like it hadn't bothered her at all. Madison wished she could be more like her. Jordan wouldn't have fallen apart at practice today.

Madison was still disappointed about it. Mrs. Albright had tried to get her mind off the competition, but Madison could not shake her unending nerves. How would she feel tomorrow? She hadn't fully explained what was going on to anyone. What if saying what her problems were made them worse? It was one thirty in the morning and Madison lay wide awake. Each time she fell asleep she had nightmares about the final round till she thrashed herself awake again.

Finally, Madison firmly told herself everything was fine. She repeated it until she dozed off, but slept fitfully through the night.

Luckily, the start time for the long program was not at dawn. When the alarm buzzed, she turned over and relaxed. She checked her voicemail. A message from an ecstatic Jordan raved about how much fun she'd had at the fair. She closed the message by wishing Madison good luck. Jordan assured Madison she was a great skater, even though she had only seen her skate once or twice. Madison smiled. That's what friends were for, right?

While her mom slept in, Madison showered, glad to be alone with her thoughts. She felt much better, like a weight had been lifted off. Soon Mrs. Albright knocked on the door.

"Come in," Madison called, combing her hair. Her mother poked her head in.

"Morning, sweetheart," she said sleepily and gave Madison a hug. "I'll help you with your make-up in a minute."

Madison felt her stomach flip-flop as she pictured herself dressed and made up to compete, though she flashed her mom an upbeat smile. *I'm not showing any nerves today,* Madison decided.

"Glad to see you're feeling better. Now, let's apply that make-up."

Mrs. Albright worked fast, the foundation and blush applied at lightening speed. The eyes came next. In no time, Mrs. Albright wheeled Madison around to face the mirror.

"Ta-da," she said proudly.

Madison smiled, thinking *Good.* This time Mrs. Albright had used greens and golds to offset Madison's pink costume.

"Thanks, mom." Madison said appreciatively.

Mrs. Albright checked her watch. "We'd better go. Throw on your clothes and let's head downstairs. We have to be out the door in five minutes."

Madison scurried to get dressed while her mom rushed around. Mrs. Albright carried the costume bag, Madison grabbed her skates, and they were off.

Madison ignored the other skaters in the hotel lobby. She grabbed a light breakfast and stepped outside. She shivered; fall had arrived.

Heading to the arena, Madison grew anxious. Once inside, Madison pushed through the crowd to get to the locker room quickly. A fresh batch of results hung on yet another window. Once Madison started warming up, she was in a trance, running, stretching, and walking through her moves. She tensed each time she walked through her double axel and triple toe. *Relax,* she commanded herself. Suddenly, Madison felt a tap on her shoulder. She jumped and turned around.

"Whoa, relax would you?" Jillian laughed.

Madison pulled her earbuds out. "I couldn't hear anything. When did you get here?"

"About the same time as you. You walked right past me. But I decided not to take you ignoring me personally. You looked pretty stressed."

"Aren't you?" Madison asked absentmindedly. She was still trying to focus on her program.

Jill shrugged. "I guess so. A little. But what's the point? No matter how I skate, they are always going to tell me that I can do it better; so really I have nothing to lose."

"Jill—" Madison started.

"No, it's true. And you don't have to worry either. You're the best skater here."

"I wish people would stop telling me that."

"Why? I would love to hear that," Jillian said.

"It just makes me more nervous. Last night I was having nightmares! The judges were chasing me around on the ice and I kept falling and everyone was booing me. It's too much pressure to live up to being the best." She furrowed her brow. "Or at least what people *think* is the best."

Jillian slung an arm around Madison. "Don't sweat it. You just have to go skate. In an hour it will all be over, anyway."

"True."

"And if you blow it, nobody will remember."

"Thanks, Jill. I think."

"I didn't mean that I think you're going to screw up." Jill corrected quickly.

"I know. I'm just nervous. I'll be fine."

Liz came up behind them. "Maddie, how are you today?"

"Hey, Liz. I'm good," Madison said as cheerfully as she could. Jillian snorted. Both Liz and Madison turned to look at her.

"Sorry," she said, "I think Maddie's just slightly more nerve-wracked than she wants you to think."

"Shut up," Madison laughed. Jillian turned and walked away, still chuckling to herself.

"What was that about?" Liz asked.

"Nothing. I had some bad dreams."

"Are you doing better than yesterday?"

"I think so."

"What do you mean, you think so?"

"Well, I don't feel as anxious. And when I woke up, I felt ready to go."

Liz looked skeptical. "Good. As long as you feel ready. Let's not have a repeat of yesterday's practice. You'd better go get changed. I'll meet you at the door."

Madison stepped into her costume. She surveyed the sparkling flower design in the mirror before zipping up her warm-up jacket. She finished a last-minute touchup on her lips and headed toward the ice.

***

The butterflies were threatening to bubble over as she approached the gate. Madison and the rest of the skaters in Group B checked in and waited. She kept herself warm as the last competitor in Group A skated. Madison heard the crowd gasp several times as the skater fell. Knowing a skater had fallen took some pressure off, but Madison preferred to win when everyone had skated her best. After she finished, the rink grew quiet for a few moments and then the announcer dismissed the previous group: "Will the next group of skaters, Intermediate Ladies Group B, please take the ice for the warm-up? Please welcome to the ice Carly Mately, Jessica James, Sarah McDonald, Alana Rimanova, Madison Albright, and Jillian Knight."

Madison tried to stay calm, but the pressure to skate perfectly was strangling her. She looked up into the stands and spotted Caitlin's pouty expression. She saw Rebecca Boyle slip into a seat. Her mom sat along the top row of the bleachers, trying to be incognito by wearing a hat and scarf.

"Madison, get moving!" Liz coached from the side of the boards. A minute had gone by and she hadn't done anything yet. Madison began warming up her spins and jumps. She executed them all successfully but weakly.

"One minute remaining in warm-up."

Madison skated a few spirals and one step sequence. She did a few laps, calming herself.

"Time. Please clear the ice," the announcer's voice echoed. Madison glanced at the stands. Her mom was biting her nails and Rebecca looked unimpressed. *They don't like the way I'm skating,* Madison thought worriedly. She followed Liz into the hall.

"Hey, it's okay," Liz said. "Your warm-up was a little shaky, but better now than in a few minutes. You're supposed to get the kinks out now." She smiled but noted Madison's distracted face. "Madison?"

"What? What?" Madison said, startled.

"Did you hear anything I just said?"

"Oh, um, yeah. You said something about the warm-up being okay."

"Yes. I also said it's good to get the kinks out now. Girl, you look spooked. What's the matter?"

"Nothing. I'm fine." Madison snapped back to attention.

"What were you thinking just now?" Liz demanded.

"Only about skating a clean program," Madison said earnestly. It was another lie, of course. Madison had imagined herself falling yet again.

Liz wasn't convinced. "Most people look happy when they picture that. You looked like you wanted to hide under a rock."

"You know me, Liz. The quieter I am before competition, the better I skate," Madison explained. Today she was quiet because she didn't know what would happen out there.

Liz's hands grasped Madison's shoulders. "Breathe. It's going to be fine. You're going to be fine. You're trained. You're ready. You are in control of what happens out there. You have the ability to skate an awesome program, but me telling you that doesn't mean much. You have to believe it for yourself. That makes all the difference." Liz waited for Madison to answer. When she remained silent, Liz asked, "Well, do you believe you can do it?"

Madison's head was screaming, *No! No, I can't! What will everyone say if I mess up?* But instead, Madison calmly stated, "Yes, I believe I can."

Liz dropped the subject, unconvinced. The two walked back into the cold arena. The third skater was already halfway through her program. Madison took her jacket off to prepare for the cold—never an easy thing. Then Liz wheeled Madison around to face away from the performer. "No watching today."

Madison knew she was right. It definitely helped to be out of earshot as the other skaters competed. If she knew the others had skated poorly, she might become too relaxed and make careless mistakes. If she knew they had skated flawlessly, she might become so tense that she couldn't perform well. She stood, trying to think only of her program.

"Go out there and have fun," Liz was saying. "That's why you do this, right? So go show everyone how much you love it." Madison nodded, but she was losing her concentration. She felt like the walls were closing in around her.

"Madison? Come on. You're on in about thirty seconds," Liz said. She gazed at Madison intently and handed her a bottle of water. "Drink," she instructed.

Madison took a sip. She was dizzy. *That's all I need,* she thought. Madison blinked her eyes hard to make the huge room stop spinning.

"Maddie, it's time."

Madison swallowed forcefully. She slipped off her guards and turned to face Liz at the boards. Liz took Madison's hands in hers. "Come on, Maddie. You can do this. Just relax."

Madison nodded but she couldn't focus. Her head was somewhere else. Liz looked concerned, but said nothing more.

"Representing the Arctic Circle Figure Skating Club, please welcome Madison Albright."

Madison stroked out and presented herself. A hush fell over the crowd as she struck her opening pose. The first strands of the Spanish guitar strummed and Madison began to skate. She was hesitant beginning each move. Even her trademark layback spin was slower than usual. But Madison had a job to do. She had already done this program perfectly in the qualifying round. She could do it again. Madison prepared for her double axel. She landed it. She expected to feel a wave of relief flood through her body, but instead she thought, *Don't screw up now. The second jump is always the hardest!* Madison rounded the corner and glimpsed Liz smiling tensely. Madison tried to express the music as she went into her triple toe. Suddenly every muscle tensed as she picked for the jump. She came down almost as quickly as she went up. She popped. *Great!* Madison thought, *now they won't even know what that jump was supposed to be.* She forced the horrified look off her face and kept going. *If I don't look upset, maybe no one else will notice how bad this is.* She blanked on what to think as she took off for her next jump. She landed the double Lutz, but singled the loop. The crowd moaned. *So they do know how badly it's going.* Madison felt tears welling up in her eyes but pushed them aside.

The slow part of her music started and Madison stepped into her spiral sequence. She pulled her leg above her head into a Biellmann position. She did a change of edge spiral. She finished her spiral sequence without any mistakes. Her combination spin was also good. Still, Madison could not relax or focus on a single thought. The triple salchow was up next. *Please let me land this!* Madison pleaded silently. She did a three-turn into the jump and took off. Suddenly she found herself on the ice. *Oh no!* Madison shrieked inside her head. It was over. She would never make the podium now. Madison fought the dizzy spell with everything she had. She executed each turn in her footwork deliberately, showing deep edges and quick feet. She landed her double flip shakily *Whatever. I'm on my feet,* she thought. *Okay, last jump. Breathe. Just do it.* Madison closed her eyes as she took off for her double loop. Not the smartest thing to do, but she figured she was so past the point of skating well it didn't really matter. She landed it. *Oh, thank goodness,* Madison thought.

The music picked up and she headed into her straight-line footwork. She was skating carefully, but at least she was getting through the program. She lifted into her flying camel—the last element. She changed edge in the middle of the spin and then lifted her leg into a split as the last part of the spin. Doing such a difficult element at the end of the program gave her higher points. She exited the spin, her arms raised in a Spanish flamenco position, and it was over.

The audience clapped. Madison dared to lift her eyes and saw that her mom was now trying to shove as many nails into her mouth as possible. Madison glanced at Rebecca's suddenly vacant seat. *Did she walk out in the middle?* Madison wondered. She skated over to Liz, who stood statue-like, giving nothing away. After a quick hug, Liz ushered her into the hallway. Madison didn't even have time to wish Jillian good luck. Madison watched as Liz paced the hallway, breathing fast. After several painful minutes, she looked at Madison, who could see the anger and disappointment in Liz's eyes.

"What happened out there?" she finally said. "Madison, I knew all my students would do well, but you were my *for sure* medal winner. You were supposed to move on to Junior Nationals."

"I know." Madison really wished Liz would stop talking.

"I don't know what to do with you. I'm used to working with people who aren't as talented as you to bring them up to their highest possible level. I'm not used to working with such a talented skater who then falls apart at competition. I don't understand why this happened. Everything was fine in qualifying."

"Liz, I...."

Liz put up a hand. "Stop. You couldn't explain what was going on before; don't try now. Why don't you go get changed? We'll check the results and go from there." Liz walked away.

Madison was too stunned to move. The day's events came back with sudden clarity. *What did I just do?* she thought angrily as she carelessly tossed her skates into her bag. She had had it with skating and the competition. Madison quickly wiped her eyes with the back of her hand as Jillian walked in.

"How did it go?" Madison asked Jill casually.

"Oh, okay. I fell twice. I don't think I'll be making it out of the region." Jill responded gloomily.

"Well, did your other elements make up for the falls?" Madison offered sympathetically.

Jillian half-smiled. "I don't think so."

"Are you okay?" Madison asked. She remembered what Jillian's mom had threatened before the start of the competition.

Jillian looked up at the ceiling. "I think so. I don't think my mom will really make me quit. She wants this more than anything. Hey, this might even be a good thing. Maybe she'll blame it on my coach and then I can switch to someone else."

"Always positive."

"You bet," Jillian said. "What about you? How did you do?"

"Don't ask."

"Come on. It can't be that bad."

"It is. I fell twice and I singled the double loop in my combination. Everything else went okay. But I doubt I'll make it out, either."

"You might because of the other stuff."

"No, I don't think so. And Liz is so mad and disappointed in me! She doesn't even want to talk to me."

"Ouch! Sometimes people have off days. Liz's reaction isn't fair."

"Maybe, but I don't mess up. Everyone expects me to be perfect. And I was at the beginning of the week and then I don't know—everything fell apart." Madison let her tears fall. She didn't care if her make-up got smeared. She wasn't perfect anymore, anyway.

"Maddie! It's okay. It'll all work out. Liz is just burning off steam." Jillian tried to console her friend.

"She has every right to be mad. I made stupid mistakes and now it's too late to fix them."

Jillian said nothing. Madison figured that deep down Jill knew Madison was right. She could tell that Jillian was happy with her own skate today. If Madison had only skated like she was capable of, she'd be that happy, too. The results wouldn't be posted for about another thirty minutes. Madison wished Jillian good luck and left.

To be alone, she went into the nearest bathroom and locked the stall door. She cried out all the emotions of the past week.

She recalled how excited she'd been that she was going to train and compete at—and maybe win—regionals. As regionals approached, she'd felt more pressure than she had bargained for. By the end of August, coaches and skaters around the rink noticed Madison's progress. At first, she enjoyed their compliments, but soon they overwhelmed her. In her fear of letting down people's expectations, she became obsessed with skating perfectly. Doubts ruined the compliments she'd received.

The regional championships were her chance to prove their high expectations were justified. *But I didn't do that, did I?* Madison thought harshly. She let those she cared about down. She'd put so much pressure on herself to be the best that she wound up skating poorly.

How long have I been in here? Time to face reality, Madison thought. She looked in the mirror to see the damage from her tears. Not too bad, considering how hard she had been crying. She wiped away the streaked mascara, reapplied her lip gloss, and patted her puffy eyes. Madison bit her lip. She couldn't stall any longer. Her biggest concern was how her mother would react. Madison had been wrong to hope for Liz's support. She hoped her mom would still be there for her. Mrs. Albright had never given Madison any reason to doubt her support, but then again Madison had never before performed poorly. Madison stepped into the lobby. She wasn't ready to look at the results yet; she wanted her mom. She quickly spotted Mrs. Albright, cell phone in hand. She saw Madison and looked relieved.

"There you are. I was just calling you. Where have you been?"

"Oh, the locker room and bathroom," Madison said casually.

"You look a little beaten down."

"How do you think I feel?" Madison snapped. Mrs. Albright gestured for Madison to sit next to her. Madison slumped onto the bench and rested her head on her mother's shoulder.

"I know you are upset. Nothing I say can change the fact that you made a few mistakes. But," her mother paused, "*I'm* proud of you. I'm proud of all your training, of you going out in front of all those people, especially after yesterday."

"Yeah, for nothing." Madison said flatly.

"Not for nothing. Maybe you won't make it out of the region this year. It's a learning experience. I saw how nervous you were before you even got on the ice. Now you know what happens when you feel like that. And you have to learn how to change it."

"That doesn't do me any good. I don't need to learn, I need to win."

"Nobody wins without making a few mistakes along the way, honey. You can't win all the time. Sometimes losing makes us more determined to fight for what we want."

"Not me. I don't ever want to skate again!" Madison sobbed.

"You say that now. Have you even checked the results?"

"No. Have you?"

"Yes, but I'm not going to tell you. Go check them."

"But it's so humiliating. I was supposed to win and now my name is going to be way down at the bottom. I don't want to see that I didn't skate well enough to go to Junior Nationals."

"You have to face it. Results are part of competition—good or bad."

"Fine," she snapped again and she stomped off in the direction of the postings. She protested, *I don't want to look. Who cares what place I got now? I wonder who won, anyway—not that it matters. I don't care.* Once she reached the posting, she was just going to find her name and move away quickly. Her eyes scanned the sheets for her level:

1. JESSICA JAMES

2. SARAH McDONALD

3. ALANA RIMANOVA

4. KATRINA MARTIN

5. MADISON ALBRIGHT

Madison stopped cold. *Fifth? Are you kidding me? I missed by one?* Her disappointment with her skate turned to anger as Madison scanned the rest of the list. Jillian had come in a respectable sixth. But Madison could only think of the unfairness of it all. It was unfair that she got the worst case of nerves ever right before she skated, unfair that she had made so many mistakes, and most definitely unfair that she missed going to Junior Nationals by just one place. She sulked back to her mom.

"See?" Mrs. Albright said. "Fifth is not so bad."

"Not so bad? *Not so bad?*" Madison tried unsuccessfully to keep her voice steady. "You do realize that I missed Junior Nationals by one place, right?"

Mrs. Albright's face fell. "Oh, I'm sorry. I thought it was top five."

"No, it's top four. But I don't deserve to go the way I skated. I'm such an idiot. Who does that? Who blows it because of nerves?"

"Lots of competitors do, Madison. You're not the only one that fell because she was nervous, I'm sure."

Madison pursed her lips. "Can we just get out of here? I want to go home."

"Don't you want to say goodbye to Liz? Maybe watch some of the other events?"

"I don't think Liz wants to say goodbye to me. I don't want to watch. Can we please go?" Madison was about to cry again.

"Why wouldn't Liz want to say goodbye to you?"

"She's mad," Madison said bitterly. "Let's just go. She'll get over it."

Mrs. Albright hesitated. "Maybe I should talk to her. Being angry isn't really the appropriate reaction for a coach. I mean, she can be disappointed, but she really shouldn't make you feel worse than you already do."

"Don't worry about it, mom. Please don't say anything. It's between Liz and me."

Mrs. Albright looked angry. "I still think you should say goodbye. It shows respect for her." She looked at Madison. Madison stared back, but after a few moments, she lost the staring contest.

"I'll go find her, but then I want to leave." Madison wandered off, but there was no sign of Liz's shoulder-length light brown hair or the red coat she always wore to competition. Instead, Madison locked eyes with Rebecca Boyle. Madison quickly dropped her gaze and tried to hurry out of the path of Rebecca's stare. Too late—she could hear Rebecca's heels sticking to the matted floor behind her.

"Madison, wait!" Rebecca called. But Madison pushed forward. Rebecca caught up to her and grabbed her arm to turn her around. She looked concerned.

"Didn't you hear me?" she asked. "How did you rank?"

"Fifth," Madison said shortly, hoping Rebecca would leave her alone.

"That's too bad. When I saw you a few weeks ago, I thought you were going to win for sure. What happened?"

Madison clucked her tongue. *Oh, could you please stop talking? Half of this is your fault for telling everyone to watch me!* "I don't know." Madison said. "I had an off day, I guess. I'll just have to do better next time."

Rebecca smiled. "That's the spirit. I'm glad you're not too upset about it. Besides, you never know what will happen during the next few weeks. The fourth-place skater was injured as this competition began. She was taking medication to numb the pain. Who knows if she'll be able to skate at Junior Nationals?"

Madison's eyes widened.

"It was nice to see you. I'll catch up with you again soon." Rebecca waved and walked away.

"See you." Madison called after her.

How does she know all this stuff? She's all over these competitions. Madison ran her fingers threw her hair. As a red coat brushed past, she remembered her reason for roaming the lobby.

"Liz? Hey, Liz."

Liz turned around. Madison blushed. Liz's stare made her uncomfortable.

"I, I, just wanted to say goodbye. We're leaving now and so, yeah," Madison stammered, then gushed, "oh, and thank you for being here this week. And my mom will pay you next week."

"I won't be home until Monday afternoon. Take some time off and think about exactly what happened here this weekend. When you get back on the ice, you'd better have your head on straight."

"Right. Thanks." *I don't think I'll be back on the ice for some time, then. The pressure never stops. First, I had to worry about skating perfectly and now I have to worry about not worrying!* Madison thought as she headed back to her mom.

"Can we go now?" Madison begged.

"Did you find Liz?"

"Yes. I don't want to talk about it right now."

Mrs. Albright stood up and gave her a hug. "Let's get out of here." With that, the two walked out of the cold arena and into the bright sunshine of an October day.

chapter

14

"I Quit"

Madison was packing the last of her bags as the hotel phone rang.

"Hey," Jillian said.

"Hi."

"Do you want to grab some lunch? I'm going soon." Jillian offered.

"No thanks. Mom and I are getting ready to leave."

"Come on, Maddie. It might help you feel better," Jillian suggested.

"Is that Jillian?" Mrs. Albright mouthed to Madison. When she nodded, Mrs. Albright waved her hand in a shooing motion. "Go," she whispered.

Madison sucked in a breath. She really didn't feel like talking to anyone, but she wasn't getting out of it. "Okay," Madison agreed reluctantly, "but it has to be quick."

"Meet you downstairs."

Minutes later the two girls left the hotel and walked to town. It was nice to explore a little bit. She hadn't had time to enjoy the neighborhood during the competition.

"I love the specialty shops here," Jillian gushed, linking arms with Madison. "Come on, let's go in here. I heard they have really good breakfast food and serve it all day."

The two grabbed a booth at the diner. Madison ordered an omelet and Jillian ordered a stack of blueberry pancakes. "What?" Jillian said in response to Madison's shocked face.

"What about all that not eating and watching what you eat? You barely ate anything this week and now you're ordering pancakes."

Jillian dismissed this statement with a casual wave of her hand. "Competition's over. My mom's not here to see. One stack of pancakes is not going to kill me...Oh, and sorry about commenting on your body before. You look great. I was just jealous and so crazy with the whole situation. No hard feelings, right?"

"Right." Madison was glad to know her earlier comments weren't what Jillian really thought about Madison's body. It still hurt that Jillian would stoop to do that, though. The girls were friends again, but Madison would never trust her like before.

"So, was your mom mad about the results?" Madison prompted.

"Yeah, she yelled at me for, like, an hour. You know, about all the money she wasted and how she was disappointed and embarrassed. And I must not be working hard enough, and on and on. Dimitri was angry, too. But he doesn't care as much as my mom. Do you know Alana Rima something? Yeah, that's his student. So he has someone going to Junior Nationals. She'll get all Dimitri's time now, so it's pretty low key for me until December."

"Are you going to switch coaches?"

"I don't know. Mom was too upset to talk about it. I'll let her cool off, then I'm going to try to switch. I hate Dimitri. There's another coach I've always wanted to take from. Hopefully, mom will let me switch."

They ate in silence. Jillian inhaled her pancakes. Madison figured she probably hadn't eaten anything substantial all week; let her enjoy them. "Wow, that was good." Jillian laughed. She took a break halfway through her stack. "So what about you? How did your mom react? Like it was no big deal, right, and she's proud of you anyway?" Resentment rose in Jillian's voice.

"Kind of." Madison didn't go into how supportive her mom was for Jillian's sake. "I don't want to talk about skating."

"It was weird. You were with it at the beginning of the week and then, poof, it was like you were in another world."

"I know and I don't get it. I don't even want to think about it."

"Yeah, and you only missed by one place," Jill said with a slight hint of satisfaction in her voice.

"Jill, stop talking about it now." Madison pushed her plate away. *Check, please.* She thought.

"Do you want to look in any of the stores?" Jillian asked, unaware of Madison's foul mood. Maybe she was trying to make up for being so mean earlier in the week. *Or,* she was relishing in Madison's defeat. Or else, seeing Madison upset made her feel better about her own situation. It angered Madison that such a thought crossed her mind about one of her friends, but Jill's recent behavior left her no choice.

"I'd love to shop, but we need to leave. I know Mom doesn't want to drive too late into the night."

Jillian shrugged. "We're staying until tomorrow. You really want to get out of here, don't you?"

"Yeah, I kinda do."

"I understand. You have to explain to all those people what happened. It's probably best to just leave and let them think you were sick or something."

They split the bill as Madison stared at Jillian. She was being extremely insensitive. Madison chalked this up to the "new Jillian." She hoped it would go away by the next time they met.

"Let's go." Madison said. Luckily, Mrs. Albright was packing up the car when the girls reached the hotel.

Jillian turned to Madison. "Well, I guess I'll leave you then."

"Yeah. Enjoy the rest of your day."

The girls hugged before Jillian whispered, "And I really am sorry about this whole week. How I acted and how you skated. I'm sorry you didn't make it out."

Madison's mom looked interested in what the girls were whispering.

"You, too. We'll do better next year, right?" Madison replied in farewell.

"Definitely. Keep in touch. See you later, Mrs. Albright."

"Bye, Jill. Take care," Mrs. Albright smiled.

Mom and daughter stood still. "Is it just me or does she sound happy that you didn't make Junior Nationals?" her mother asked.

"No, she's just…going through a lot. And she's very competitive. She's been supportive, really."

"Not all the time. She is friendly as long as you aren't doing too much better than her, correct?"

Though she didn't respond, Madison knew her mom was right. Jillian did seem supportive when Madison's skating went poorly but upset when Madison did well.

"It's part of getting older, Maddie. You'll have all different types of friendships and not all of them will be as deep and long lasting as you would like. Let's load the last bags and go."

Up in their room, Madison grabbed her skate bag and costumes. She felt like leaving them there. Reluctantly, Madison left the room, skates in hand, and walked to the car with a sense of finality. The week was over. All the anticipation and wondering had come down to one moment this morning, and Madison had ruined it. This was not the return from regionals that she had imagined. She thought she would ride home wanting more, but now she never wanted to see skates again.

"Did you tell Dad?" Madison asked.

"Yes, and he said just what I did. He's proud of you for going out there and training so hard. He is worried about how upset you are, though."

"I'm not upset!"

Mrs. Albright laughed. "Don't pretend. It's okay to be disappointed."

"I'm fine!"

"I think we should discuss it. Not today, but soon. Not talking is what led to this in the first place."

"I want to quit," Madison announced.

Mrs. Albright was silent for a long time. "I know, but in a few days you'll feel differently. You'll see."

"No," Madison said firmly. "I won't change my mind. Why should I train so hard to go out there, get nervous and stress myself out, only to screw up? I don't need that in my life. I want to be normal—to go to dances and stuff."

"Because you love skating. You can't just give up after one less-than-perfect performance. That's not what makes a champion, and that's what you told me you wanted to be. Now if you change your mind at some point, fine, but I won't let you quit because of this."

"You can't *make* me go to the rink. It's not important to me anymore. I'm not gonna really make it anyway. I'm too far behind now," Madison objected.

"Maddie, you're Intermediate. It's not too late at all."

"Yeah, well, Liz doesn't know what to do from here. That means she thinks I'm not worth training anymore."

"Liz just doesn't know how to deal with what happened today. Coaches should know how to deal with mental toughness, but they don't always. Liz will learn. She'll have to, for you."

"I'm a waste of her time. What's the use of a skater who's great in practice but can't pull it together in competition?"

Mrs. Albright sighed. "Look. We're not going to get anywhere today. Let's just get home. You can take some time off and we'll talk next week. Right now, you just need to feel everything and let it out. It's okay to cry."

That was the only cue Madison needed. She leaned back and burst into tears yet again. She wished the whole week had never happened. Thoughts of school flashed before her eyes and the tears came faster. It would be so embarrassing to tell everyone that she messed up. She thought of the puppy her dad had promised her. He still might buy her one, but she wouldn't accept it. She hadn't held up her end of the bargain, and she wouldn't be able to try again until next year.

Caitlin's face popped into her head next. She would never let Madison forget how she froze up and she would make sure the whole school wouldn't, either. Madison cried and cried while her mother drove. She was sure her mom was deeply disappointed in her, even though she was too nice to say it. Eventually Madison cried herself to sleep.

Before she knew it, they were pulling up to the last rest stop before the final stretch home. Four-and-a-half hours later, she did not feel any better; if possible, she felt worse. *I quit, I quit, I quit,* Madison repeated to herself. Even as she said the words, the thought of the fourth-place skater dropping out of Junior Nationals crossed her mind. Maybe she would get the chance to prove what she could do in a few weeks time.

Madison pushed these thoughts far out of her head. *It's not worth it. You can't do it. You get too nervous. Forget it,* she thought. Back in the car, she settled in for the last hour of the ride. She hadn't said anything to her mom since those first minutes of the drive and she wasn't planning to. She was cried out for now, but surely there were plenty tears left to shed. She closed her eyes and tried to sleep. At least when she rested, she didn't think.

15

Facing the Family

The car pulled into the Albrights' driveway a few hours after dark. Madison lifted her head to see the faint outline of home in the car's headlights. She banged her head on the back of the seat.

"You're awake."

"Yes, unfortunately. I feel like we just left Minnesota."

"About seven hours ago. I made a few stops to stretch my legs, but you didn't budge. Do you feel any better?" Mrs. Albright asked worriedly.

"No."

Mrs. Albright sighed. "I bet Dad and Dylan will be glad we're home."

"Dylan won't care. I don't really want to see him. He's going to make fun of me."

"He's your brother!" Mrs. Albright protested.

"Whatever."

Mr. Albright appeared outside as soon as he heard the door open.

"There are my girls!" he boomed and scooped Madison's mom into a big hug. Madison got out of the car reluctantly and was swept into a great big hug as well.

"I missed you guys." Mr. Albright began unloading the bags. Madison's dad always made a big deal when she returned from competition, but his look showed he was trying to be extra supportive this time. He didn't ask how things went or how Madison was feeling. Clearly, Mrs. Albright had briefed him and ordered him to act as if nothing were wrong. He toted the bags into the house with a smile plastered on his face.

Madison trudged upstairs holding her backpack. In Dylan's room the music was blasting as always. She tiptoed past, hoping Dylan wouldn't hear her. She was just turning the knob in her own door when a mass of brown hair poked out the door down the hall.

"Hey," it said.

"Hi," Madison pushed the door open and quickly shut it. Seconds later Dylan was in her room.

"Get out!" Madison screamed.

"Cool it. I just wanted to know if we were getting a puppy."

"Well," Madison sat up straight on her bed, eyes blazing, "if we were getting a puppy it would be *mine* not *yours,* and you know perfectly well that's not happening. You're just trying to make me feel worse."

"Have it your way," Dylan shrugged. "I just thought you could use a little support. The puppy was my opening joke."

"Not funny."

"If you don't want my help, I'll leave."

"Would you please? I have to face all the kids at school tomorrow. They're gonna make so much fun of me when they find out I stink."

"Stop being so dramatic. They might not even remember that you went to competition."

"They'll remember. The school made an announcement and everything."

Dylan turned to leave. "It's not gonna be as bad as you think." He paused and turned back to face Madison. "You work really hard. You'll get it next time."

Madison bit her lip. "Thanks Dylan. That was nice."

Dylan grinned sheepishly. "Yeah, well, don't get used to it."

Madison laid down on the bed. Now wasn't the time to tell him that she was quitting; not after he had been so nice. Madison moved in slow motion that evening. They'd arrived home too late to sit down for a family dinner—to mom's disappointment and Madison's relief. From her room she heard her parents drag the bags upstairs and begin unpacking.

She could hear Mrs. Albright describe everything about Minnesota. She heard Liz's name mentioned a few times. Mrs. Albright was furious with how Liz reacted to Madison's performance. The music blared from Dylan's room.

Madison lay staring at the ceiling, with no energy to unpack. She'd simply stuffed her skate bag in the back of the closet. Finally, the music subsided in Dylan's room and the room darkened. There was a knock on her door and her mom walked in.

"You didn't unpack."

"I didn't feel like it....Mom, do I have to go to school tomorrow?" She already knew the answer, but maybe her parents would be extra sympathetic.

"Yes," Mrs. Albright answered without hesitation. 'The longer you wait, the harder it will be. Just get it over with. But remember, how many kids in your class can say they skate, let alone compete at regionals? Can any say they made the top five? Don't forget that you are among the top five in the region. I know you wanted more, but that is pretty impressive."

"Maybe, but it's not enough. And I skated badly. I probably didn't even deserve to be where I am." Madison steadfastly held her view. She's failed to accomplish what she set out to do. Therefore, the week had been a failure; nothing anyone could say would change her mind.

"I see your take on this is no better than a few hours ago. You have to go to school tomorrow and you have to act like you had a great time. Saying that you are in the top five will still impress people, if that's what you're worried about. I won't ask them to announce anything. By Tuesday the whole competition will be behind you."

Madison crossed her arms. "I want to skip school."

"No. And don't try your dad when he comes in here, either. We already discussed it and we're not backing down."

Madison rubbed her eyes. "Then at least let me get some sleep so I can be ready."

"By all means," Mrs. Albright said sarcastically. "I only came in to give you a pep talk." She closed the door.

"Night, mom." Madison called. "Love you." *Except I hate you for making me go to school tomorrow.*

111

As Madison finished washing her face and brushing her teeth, her dad entered the room.

"Maddie, I'm gonna turn in. You'd better too. You have to get up early."

"I know." Madison showed her annoyance.

"I'll drive you."

"Okay." Madison didn't mind the offer, but she hoped he wasn't going to try to talk to her about skating.

Her dad sat on the edge once she settled in bed. He wrapped her up into another big hug. They remained quiet. If she spoke, Madison might cry, and she didn't want her dad to worry about her all night. When they let go, Mr. Albright said, "I'll see you in the morning. Love you, sweetie."

"Love you too, Dad."

Mr. Albright turned the light out as he left, and Madison resumed planning her approach to tomorrow. Her parents were trying to make her feel better and were still proud of her. But Madison was so disappointed she could not see anything there was to be proud of; maybe they were lying to her about how good she still was. She wished someone would tell her the truth: she'd messed everything up and failed. No one understood. Liz did not understand why she got so nervous, and her parents didn't realize how disappointing it was not to skate her best and not to progress from the region. They assumed she would make nationals next year—no big deal. They did not understand how seriously Madison took skating and how short-lived the competitive years are for figure skaters. Jordan might understand, but Madison doubted it. Jordan would put a positive spin on the situation. The only skating goal she urged Madison to achieve was to beat the pants off Caitlin. Mission accomplished, but this time placing higher than Caitlin wasn't enough for Madison. She tried to sleep.

Tomorrow morning would arrive too fast.

16

School Blues

"Madison, get up." Mrs. Albright shouted through the door the next morning. Madison stubbornly stayed in bed.

"No."

Mrs. Albright pounded on the door. "I'm not standing for this Maddie. I told you last night you have to go to school and I'm not changing my mind."

"You can't make me."

"Oh, yes she can." Mr. Albright had joined his wife outside Madison's door. "Come on and get ready. We'll take you in your pajamas if we have to."

Madison remained silent.

"The longer you stay in there, the later you will be. I will not tell the school to excuse the absence. Then you'll have a cut class on your record." Mrs. Albright tried again.

This got Madison's attention. She prided herself on having near-perfect attendance as well as good grades. Madison reasoned, *I could let one day go, especially under these circumstances. I've got a good excuse.* Madison's silence clearly had her parents baffled. She never disobeyed them like this. Madison overheard her mom tell her dad that this was what middle school girls were like and if he thought this was bad, he should just wait until she got into high school.

"I'm not going." She yelled through the door.

"Yes you are young lady. We aren't giving you a choice. Now get dressed." Her dad shouted back. He rarely raised his voice. Madison was pushing her luck, but she remained in bed.

She heard more murmurs and another door open. A pair of feet scrambled downstairs. *They've given up,* she thought triumphantly. Madison was gloating as she stretched out on her bed. She rolled over onto her stomach, relieved that she didn't have to deal with school today. She heard her door open a crack.

Closing her eyes, she pretended to fall back asleep. Suddenly Madison heard a sound like a faucet running, then *splash!*

"Yikes! Dylan, I'm gonna kill you!" Madison ran after her brother, pulling at her soaking wet shirt as Dylan howled with laughter, holding an empty glass of water. Madison grabbed another shirt and ran to the bathroom, passing her hysterical parents in the hallway. When she emerged ten minutes later, the three were still laughing.

"What'd you do that for?" Madison threw Dylan a dirty look.

"I got tired of you all screaming. You were waking me up and I was annoyed. I knew the water would get you out of bed."

"It was freezing," Madison said indignantly. A smile, then a giggle, and then a full-blown laugh escaped Madison's mouth.

"And it got you laughing," her dad pointed out.

Madison had forgotten her problem for a moment, but her dad's comment brought it all back. She grew somber.

"Are you ready?" Mrs. Albright asked, sensing Madison's shifting mood.

"I guess so." Madison grabbed her backpack and headed into the kitchen. She took a banana and ate in silence.

Mr. Albright walked in and said, "The car's ready when you are."

"I am." Madison looked at her mom, who gave her an encouraging smile. Madison rolled her eyes and stomped out of the house. Once they had pulled out of the driveway, Mr. Albright handed Madison a piece of paper.

"What's this?" she asked. "It's just a triangle with stick figures."

"It's not a triangle; it's a pyramid." Mr. Albright said cheerfully.

"Dad, if this has to do with regionals—" Madison began. "It does, but it also has to do with your future. You need to hear this, so listen up." Madison stared back at the triangle. The bottom row of stick figures was divided into two halves. "The bottom layer represents all the kids in the country your age. That layer with lots of stick figures shows the kids who don't skate. The second layer shows the kids that do. There are a lot more in that bottom layer for nonfigure skaters, right?"

Madison nodded, not really sure where he was going with this.

"That second layer shows the figure skaters. See that already you are doing a sport that not many people can do. Now look at the third layer—not as many stick people, right? That shows the level of skater where you are now. There are still a lot of competitors, but not as many. Now see the next stripe? That represents junior and senior skaters; it has just a few figures, right? And the very top layer—just the tip of the pyramid—represents skaters getting to worlds and the Olympics. There are only five figures in that top layer." Mr. Albright was proud of his pyramid, but Madison was lost.

"So you're trying to show me that hardly anybody makes it and I'm not going to be one of the lucky ones?" Madison suggested.

"No, just the opposite. A lot of kids have success at your age and younger, but it gets harder as you get older. People quit because they get hurt, or they don't want to work hard, or they don't like the commitment. But with your talent and drive, if you keep at it, you can be one of the people at the top."

"How? I'm not even first at regionals now."

"Madison, this pyramid is supposed to show you that at Intermediate level, you are still in a large group of competitors. Now is not the time one competition will make or break your skating career." He pointed to the middle of the pyramid. "See how many people have success down here, where you are? They fizzle out. They usually can't sustain their success. It's not about one competition. It's about getting better and staying with it." He pointed to the top of the pyramid. "Staying in skating that far is where the success really matters. If you stick with it, that can be you."

"I don't think so."

"If you want to be a champion, you're going to have some setbacks along the way. It's handling them that makes you good. If you run away, you'll never get what you want. In the big picture of your skating career, this week's setback is not a big deal. It only feels like it because this is your first major disappointment. Believe me, if you're serious about skating there will be plenty more. You have to fight through them."

"Why would I want to do something that's going to cause me so much hurt and frustration?" Madison asked as they pulled up to school.

"Because everything worthwhile can be painful and frustrating—especially activities you love most."

"Wait." Mr. Albright handed her the pyramid. "Bring it with you. Think about it."

Madison pursed her lips and grabbed the paper. "Love you," Mr. Albright mouthed. Madison returned the gesture.

Miraculously entering her classroom just as the homeroom bell rang. Madison tried to hide in her seat. The loudspeaker crackled as the day's announcements began. The very last announcement caught Madison's attention.

"And let's congratulate Caitlin on her recent skating accomplishments. She placed tenth out of one hundred and forty-five skaters at last weekend's regional championships. Congratulations, Caitlin."

Tenth? Madison thought. *Try fifth!* A moment of regret at not announcing her results surged through Madison. She quickly reminded herself that any announcement would likely lead to unwanted questions. She felt a tap on her left shoulder. Madison stiffened slightly as she remembered Peter and his nosiness before the competition.

"Hey, ice skater. What's up?"

"Not much. You?"

"The same as always. The Halloween fair was cool, though. I won the best costume."

"Great, what did you go as?" Madison pretended to be interested.

"A Porsche. I made my whole costume look like the inside of the car. It made engine noises and it had a horn you could beep."

"How creative," Madison was only half listening.

"Yeah." Peter missed the sarcasm. "But it probably wasn't as cool as your weekend was. How was Minnesota?"

"Small town, lots of skaters. The weekend went pretty fast." *Please don't ask,* she pleaded silently.

Peter laughed. "Not surprised about the small town. But how was the competition?"

Madison tried to act causal. "It was fine. I skated and that was it."

"Yeah, but how did you do? What place did you get?" Peter pressed on.

Madison inhaled and exhaled slowly. "It went all right. I came in fifth."

"Is that good?"

"It depends on your definition of good."

"Well it's good to me. I've seen some of the stuff you guys do. It's pretty nuts."

"Yeah, and it's getting crazier every year. We don't just have to skate now, we have to be acrobats as well."

"I'm happy it went well for you. Or at least I think I it did, but I don't know much about skating. Still on your way to the Olympics, I guess."

Madison flinched. Nobody knew how badly placing fifth threw her. She seemed to be the only one disappointed with how regionals went, with the exception of Liz. Maybe she shouldn't feel this bad. Madison massaged her temples, confused. When the bell rang signaling time to change classes, Jordan immediately bounded over to Madison, her eyes wide.

"Did you hear that announcement about Caitlin? Ha! The whole time I was thinking that you were sitting there probably having won the whole event and no one's even mentioning it."

"I didn't win."

"Second, then?"

They slid into their seats for second period. The girls sat next to each other in almost every class.

"I got fifth," Madison said dejectedly.

"Hey, you beat Caitlin," Jordan cackled as predicted.

"Caitlin didn't even make final round. She got tenth in qualifying."

"How did you do in qualifying?"

"I won my group."

"That's awesome," Jordan said encouragingly.

"Maybe, but I didn't make it out of the region. I missed by one place."

"That part stinks," Jordan whispered as class started. "Is there any way you can go to Junior Nationals?"

"Only if one of the girls withdraws," Madison explained.

Mrs. Sharp glared at the girls and they opened their books. Madison's mind was elsewhere again. Rebecca did say that the fourth-place skater had been injured. *This isn't the way I wanted to get invited to Junior Nationals, but…I decided to quit,* Madison debated. *Don't even think of someone getting hurt.*

All that school day, Madison fought a constant battle in her mind between quitting and hoping to win a slot at Junior Nationals. She stayed close by Jordan during lunch and passing periods, as if Jordan somehow offered protection from the stares and questions aimed at Madison. At least twenty people asked her how she did and what her skating plans were. With each answer, the hurt grew. By the end of the school day, Madison felt like someone had punched her in the stomach, knocking the wind out of her.

Jordan tried to cheer her up. Madison's only funny story to tell was Dylan dousing her with water this morning. Madison wondered whether Jordan had a crush on Dylan, judging from the way she laughed at Madison's story. Madison grinned. It was near impossible to keep up with Jordan and her many beaus.

"I didn't call all weekend because I thought you'd be celebrating," Jordan was explaining as the girls walked home.

"I didn't call because I was depressed."

"Oh, Maddie!"

"How was the fair?" Madison asked, changing the subject. She didn't really want to get Jordan down. "I don't even know what happened."

"Well," Jordan's expression brightened. "I called Tyler right after I hung up with you. I told him he had asked me out first, which means that it was my right to go with him. *And* I added that he must like me better if I was his first choice."

"Wow!"

"Then I told him that I could easily take someone better and he practically begged me to go with him all over again. And we had a great time." Jordan finished with flourish, "We're going to the movies this weekend."

"Are you gonna start ditching me for guys now?" Madison joked.

"No, of course not." Jordan looked offended, but then joked back, "Not all the time...but he's so cute and so funny and so smart and...."

"Good."

"We need to get you one," Jordan said suddenly.

"One what?"

"A boyfriend. That's exactly what you need." Jordan was confident that going to a movie or a dance with a cute boy was enough to cure any ill.

"What I need is to reskate last week."

"No, what you *need* is to get over last week." Jordan looked at her with the one eyebrow she always raised whenever she wanted to make a clear point.

"I don't know...."

"You know Peter? I think he likes you. Maybe you could go out with him?" Jordan suggested.

"I don't like him like that." Madison was firm in her decision. She felt no butterflies—or slugs either—when she looked at Peter.

"So? Just go out with him. Maybe you'll change your mind."

"I doubt it."

"Think about it. Seriously Maddie, you need to lighten up."

"So I've been told."

"Well this is me, your best friend, telling you." Jordan said. "Think about it."

"I will. See ya."

"See ya." Jordan called over her shoulder.

Madison and Jordan parted ways. New thoughts brewed in Maddie's head, *Peter is kinda cute. It can't hurt to see him a few times, and it would make Peter happy.* Madison had never had a boyfriend. She'd never had time. But today was the start of her new life without skating. She would have a lot of time on her hands now and a boyfriend would fill some gaps. *And* she would have someone to go to dances and parties and movies with. Madison slipped quietly into her house and crept into her bedroom. She needed a nap. She didn't feel as excited about her new life as at first. She refused to worry about it, however. *This is what I want,* she thought. *I chose not to skate anymore and I'm fine with it.* Madison guessed she'd see how fine she really was in a few days.

17

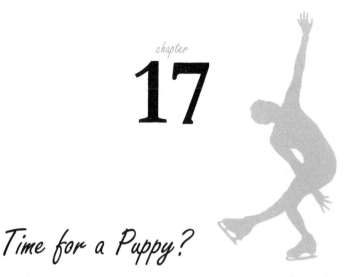

Time for a Puppy?

Madison slowly opened her eyes as she was gently shaken awake.

"It's dinner time. We'd really like you to eat with us tonight," Mr. Albright said.

Madison, still groggy from her nap, was too tired to refuse. Besides, she didn't have to talk at dinner; she just had to sit at the table. Her mom, dad, and Dylan were still energized from their day. Madison, wearing her oldest and comfiest pajamas, appeared still half asleep.

"Nice jammies," Dylan commented.

"Shut up," said Madison plopping into her regular seat. Mr. and Mrs. Albright exchanged glances. Tonight was shaping up to be a rough night at the dinner table. Mom had made fish tacos, another of Madison's favorites. She was grateful. If there was any night she needed comfort food, it was tonight.

"So how was school?" Mr. Albright asked no one in particular.

Dylan and Madison both waited for the other to speak first. Madison was usually the first to crack, but tonight she steadfastly kept her mouth shut. Finally, Dylan broke the silence.

"It was fine. They're offering an ACT prep class after school on Thursdays. I'm probably gonna go."

"Dylan, wow, we didn't even have to ask!" Mrs. Albright beamed. "How did you decide all on your own?"

Dylan furrowed his brow, then shrugged. "I wanted my pick of schools," he said as if it was obvious. Madison knew

121

Dylan had chosen this topic on purpose. Any mention of ACTs or college totally engrossed their parents. Sure enough, they launched into a series of questions. They could go on for hours, so Madison was free to eat her dinner in silence.

Madison cleaned her plate first, but Mrs. Albright's rule was that no one be excused from the table until the whole family was done eating. Madison observed everyone's plates. They were in the homestretch.

"So Maddie, are you ready to pick out our new addition?" her father asked.

"What?" Madison asked as her mom choked, then coughed, on a piece of bread.

"The puppy of course."

"Uh-oh, he said it," Dylan muttered.

Madison sputtered, "I Dad, I don't want, um…I didn't hold up my end of the bargain."

"I promised we'd see what the stipulations were. Coming in first doesn't have to be the only reason to get a dog. We can get one because we want one, or because you deserve one for working hard. Or maybe just because I know you want one and I love you."

"Thanks, but I really wouldn't feel right about it. I haven't earned the dog, so I don't want it."

"You are not to be punished for not placing as high as you wanted, do you understand?" Mr. Albright stated firmly.

"It's not a punishment; it's a reality. The deal was, if I won, I'd get a puppy. I didn't win, so I don't get a dog."

"Next competition then. No pressure."

"Next time I win *anything*. There will be no more skating events. I quit." Madison announced.

Silence. The announcement had the desired effect. Mrs. Albright abruptly began clearing plates. Mr. Albright looked uncomfortable.

Only Dylan looked directly at Madison and laughed. "Don't be stupid. You're not really gonna quit."

"Yes I am," Madison retorted. "Liz gave me this week off to think and I did. I don't want to skate anymore."

"Because you fell down a few times and still placed miles ahead of everybody else?" Dylan challenged.

"No because I didn't make my goal and I let everybody down."

"Nobody is as upset as you," Dylan said. "I think you're being a baby."

"I am not being a baby. I'm gonna call and tell Liz at the end of the week."

"You mean you haven't called her yet?" Dylan's eyes widened. "Then you're not gonna do it. If you were really serious, you would have done it already."

"It's only Monday," Madison shot back. "She's not even home yet."

Dylan shook his head, "You're acting like this is the end of the world. You're moping, you won't let dad buy a dog—which I want by the way—and now you're gonna quit? Geeze, Maddie, you've got problems. You better work 'em out or you're right, you'll never be able to skate again."

Now it was Madison's turn to be speechless. Dylan left without another word. Mr. Albright still looked uncomfortable and Mrs. Albright finished clearing dishes even quicker.

"May I be excused?" Madison finally managed to get out. Both her parents nodded and Madison raced up the stairs. No music blared from Dylan's room. The light was out. That meant Dylan had gone straight to sleep. Dylan did that only when he was really upset or angry.

Madison was puzzled. Why did he care so much what she did? He had never taken an interest in her skating before and now, when things were going badly, he suddenly offered an opinion. Madison felt angry, certainly, but she felt another emotion that she couldn't quite place gnawing in the back of her head. Maybe Dylan had been right about some things. But every time Madison thought about getting back on the ice, all she felt was pain. She still visualized herself skating from time to time. She'd never had to go back and look at what went wrong before. The nagging idea struck her, *Maybe I wouldn't be able to fix what went wrong. Or maybe I wouldn't get that nervous again. Or maybe I would be great in practice and then disappoint everyone in competition.*

She saw two options: She could walk away and never have to endure that disappointment again; or she could work through her nerves and risk the same result again. *Maybe I'm just not ready to decide,* she thought.

18

A Date for Madison

"So what do I have to do to get Peter to ask me out?" Madison asked Jordan at their lockers the next day.

"You really want to?"

Madison nodded slowly. "I'm leaning toward not skating anymore. So I figured a boyfriend would be a good distraction while I get used to having all that extra time."

Jordan put up a hand. "Wait, you're quitting? *That's* why you want a boyfriend?"

"I'm *thinking* of quitting. I just thought it might be good to try some of that normal middle school stuff out before I make my decision."

"Don't be too hasty, girl! You shouldn't quit. You love it too much and you're good."

"Whatever," Madison said. "Let's get back to Peter. Tell me what I have to do."

Jordan proudly told Madison everything she knew about flirting: How to look at him right, when to toss her hair, and how to ask questions to appear interested in Peter. Before Madison was ready and Jordan had finished talking, the five-minute warning bell sounded and the girls took their seats.

The homeroom bell rang and the rest of the class filed in. Madison saw Peter sit behind her. Jordan grinned. Madison felt butterflies rising in her stomach and tried to plan what she'd say, but she was drawing a blank. *I don't really want to do this,* Madison thought. The announcements were already on. Time was ticking. Madison began to fidget in her seat. *What am I gonna say? What am I gonna say?* Madison

125

jumped when she felt the familiar tap on her shoulder. Then she relaxed. Peter really liked her. Still, Madison wasn't sure she felt right; she was kind of using Peter. She pushed the thought out of her mind. Lots of girls went around finding boyfriends this way.

"How's it going?" Peter said.

"Oh, it's great." Madison remembered to sound positive and upbeat. "How are you?"

"Same old. Halloween's over and not much is going on."

"Yeah, I kind of missed Halloween, but there's always next year."

"Well, soon it will be cold enough that you can skate outside."

"Oh." Madison answered. She didn't really want to explain how skaters usually don't practice on outside rinks. Awkward silence fell. Madison panicked. *What am I gonna say? We have nothing in common!*

"So, you like cars?" Madison threw out there.

"Yeah, I love 'em. I'm going to have my own dealership someday. Only selling the best cars though. Ferrari—red, right?"

"Yeah, that's a great car," Madison said, but thought, *I wonder what it looks like.*

"Really—you like it? Most girls don't know anything about Ferraris."

"I know a little," Madison replied, dying inside.

"Yeah, well it's cool that a girl can be into cars too." Peter was quiet for a moment.

"Hey," he said hesitantly, "do you want to go bowling with me and my friends Saturday?"

That was her cue. "Sure. Sounds great."

"Yes," said Peter, blushing furiously. "I can't wait. See you tomorrow." Peter swaggered out of the classroom.

"So?" Jordan demanded, rushing over to Madison.

"We're going out Saturday," Madison said in wonder.

"Why are you surprised? I told you he likes you." Jordan rolled her eyes.

"Yeah, but it was just so easy."

"And it only gets easier from here."

126

Madison nodded. It wasn't how easy getting a date had been that baffled her. She felt guilty for letting Peter think she liked him. Plus, she had felt butterflies for something other than a skating event. Maybe it would not be as easy as Madison had thought to avoid those feelings altogether.

Madison was still ahead with school assignments, meaning she would have almost every afternoon to herself this week. She and Jordan walked home together as they had before Madison started skating everyday.

"You're so quiet." Jordan observed." You don't still feel bad about Peter do you? Just wait till you break up with him, you'll feel even worse."

"It shouldn't even get to that point."

"Trust me, Maddie, you need this. Especially if you quit—which I don't think you should," Jordan gave her a knowing look. "But if you do, you need to get used to life without skating as quickly as possible. This will help."

"My mom might not let me go."

"Then don't tell her. Just tell her you're seeing a group of kids from school—which you are."

"I can't lie about it!" Madison exclaimed.

"Whatever. But if you think she'll say no, you should skip the part about it being a date."

Madison just sighed. If this was what she had to do to date, the whole ordeal was already too stressful. Finally, she replied, "I'll think about it. See you tomorrow."

Mrs. Albright was in the kitchen when Madison stepped inside.

"Hi, hon," welcomed Mrs. Albright, stirring something wonderfully appetizing on the stove. "How was school?"

Madison shrugged and rummaged for a snack.

"Fine," she said peeling an orange. "I'm still ahead in all my classes. So I have most afternoons off homework this week."

"That can be good and bad," Mrs. Albright laughed. "It might give you too much time to think."

"I won't have *so* much time," Madison said coyly.

"Oh, really?" Mrs. Albright put a lid on her pot and sat down opposite Madison. "I'm listening."

"Well," Madison began, choosing her words carefully, "a boy in my class, Peter, really likes me. He asked me out to bowl with him and his friends and I said yes."

"And do you like Peter?"

"Of course I do." Madison squirmed and tried to avoid her mother's gaze. "Why else would I say yes?"

Mrs. Albright propped her elbows on the table. "Well, let's see. I've never heard you mention him before and you don't look very excited about it."

"I'm excited," Madison cut in.

"So tell me about him."

Madison grasped for anything she could remember about Peter. "He sits behind me. He has blond hair and blue eyes. He's okay looking and he, um, loves cars."

"And?" Mrs. Albright prompted.

"He wants to own his own car dealership someday." That was it. Madison had exhausted all she knew about Peter.

"And based only on okay looks and his interest in cars, you decided to go out with him?'

"Well, yeah," Madison replied quietly. Mom was on to her.

"Do you really like this boy or are you just trying to have something to do with your extra time? Have you already agreed to go somewhere with him?"

"Yes. On Saturday night." Madison blushed. Telling her mom made Madison feel much worse about what she was doing to Peter. "But so what? I don't have to like him as long as he likes me. Can't I just try dating? He probably won't even realize I don't like him."

"When he does realize it, you'll hurt him. A person shouldn't be just a distraction from your troubles."

"What, are you just not going to let me go?" Madison asked defiantly.

"No, I'll leave that up to you as long as his mother drives you there and back. But I think it's a mistake and a rotten way to treat Peter."

"Mom, it's not going to be as bad as you think. I can always find a way out of more dates without hurting his feelings. And who knows, I might really like him."

"You have a few days to decide." Mrs. Albright pursed her lips, meaning she was done discussing the date. "Liz should be back. Are you going to call her today?"

"Maybe I'll wait a few more days. She's probably so stressed with just getting back. I'll give her some time to relax first."

"I'd have thought that you would want to get it over with, telling her you're quitting."

"She doesn't care," Madison said bitterly. "She doesn't know what to do with me anymore."

"She shouldn't have said that to you." Liz's comment still upset Mrs. Albright.

"But she did. And now it's too late for her to take it back."

"I don't think she really meant it," Mrs. Albright started, but Madison didn't wait for her to finish.

The tears were welling up. Madison stomped up the stairs. Madison didn't want to admit how much Liz giving up on her had hurt her. She cried for a few minutes and then forced herself to stop, deciding *I will not get upset about Liz and skating anymore. The more I get upset, the harder it will be to get over.* She pulled out a book. Madison loved to read because it took her away from her daily life. She could forget about everything but the characters if she could clear her head. She couldn't. The book was no match for her thoughts.

Liz's words kept replaying: "I don't know what to do with you, Madison." Those words haunted Madison. Without Liz's faith and encouragement, Madison could go nowhere in the sport. All skaters need a coach who pushes them through the bad as well as good times.

Madison thought briefly of switching coaches, but she didn't want things to end on a bad note with Liz. Madison went downstairs and turned on the TV, with the volume loud in an attempt to drown out her thoughts. Flipping channels, she came across Skate America, the first competition in the Grand Prix series. She couldn't tear her eyes away from the screen or force her fingers to change the channel, although it was painful to watch. Her favorite skaters were warming up. Madison felt a stab of sadness, remembering her dream of being just like them. She clicked the TV off angrily. She walked past the kitchen without saying a word to her mother, but Madison could feel her mother's knowing stare follow her all the way up to her bedroom.

19

Time on Her Hands

The week wore on. Madison was disappointed that so much of what she studied was a review of materials from previous years. Nothing was sparking an interest.

Jordan, on the other hand, could care less about school subjects. The only subject she was fascinated with was Tyler, and she rattled on to Madison about him. Madison had more facts floating around in her head about Tyler Shaw than she had algebra equations. Madison had her own share of boy business. Peter still tapped her on the shoulder every morning and talked to her during homeroom. Jordan took this as a sign that things were moving along beautifully and couldn't stop telling Madison how awesome Saturday would be.

Madison had different feelings toward the date. As Saturday approached, she became more and more anxious. Her mom hadn't said anything about the date plans, but she made little comments and looks that let Madison know she disapproved. Nobody in the family had mentioned her skating, either. Talk around the dinner table focused more on Dylan. Nobody even bothered to ask Madison what she planned to do about skating. It peeved Madison slightly. Didn't anybody care she'd quit, or had they all given up on her, like Liz?

Not only was Madison annoyed, but her body was starting to stiffen up as well. She was used to exercising hard six days a week, but this week she had barely moved. She wasn't hungry, either. Without the workouts, Madison felt no need to eat. She could see her mother's growing concern over this issue. Mrs. Albright was sure Madison was not eating in an attempt to stay thin. This was partially true, but Madison didn't like to admit that to anyone.

By Friday, Madison thought she was seriously going out of her mind from boredom, she had so much extra time on her hands. Still, Madison surged ahead with plans for her life without skating. Eventually she would get used to having all the extra time, wouldn't she? Once she made new friends and discovered new hobbies, she would have less free time or would be as busy as she was before, just with different activities. She was determined to be excited about her date Saturday night. Wasn't this way better than living with the pressure and worry that skating had put on her? Madison was relieved when Friday morning finally came. Peter tapped her on the shoulder in homeroom as usual.

"I can pick you up at your house tomorrow, right?" Peter asked. "It would be good to meet your parents. I mean I've seen them with you at school events, but it will be great to get to know them as your boyfriend." Peter grinned.

"Boyfriend?" Madison's voice quivered.

"Well when you go on a date that's what you are," Peter laughed, clearly thinking she was playing around.

"Right, ha-ha." Madison laughed weakly.

"Is seven okay?"

"Yes."

"See you tomorrow," said Peter, gently brushing his hand on hers. He walked away before Madison could say anything.

"What was that?" Jordan asked. Madison hoped that no one had noticed, but it seemed Peter's feelings toward her were obvious.

"I don't know," Madison squeaked, "he called himself my boyfriend. I just agreed to go out, not to be a couple."

"He must really like you if he's already calling you his girlfriend."

"But I never said he could!" Madison exclaimed. "I don't want him to be my boyfriend. I just wanted to try dating."

"Don't sweat it. Guys change like the wind. By tomorrow he could be calling someone else his girlfriend," Jordan laughed. "But he *really* seems to like you. It might be harder to get out of this one."

"Great," Madison muttered. The only bright spot in this little dilemma was that it took her mind off skating. All day Friday she thought about Peter and what would happen on their date. Madison took her time walking home from school. She did not want to tell Mrs. Albright what Peter had said but knew she couldn't hide the day's events from her mom.

"You are so slow," Jordan complained. "What's up with that?"

"I guess I'm just getting out of shape really fast," Madison tried to joke.

"Oh, Maddie. If you miss it so much why don't you just go back to it again?" Jordan snapped.

"Miss what?"

"You know what. This whole week you've been miserable and you're dragging me down. You have a real negative energy."

"That's not true," Madison clenched her fists. "Peter likes me. He asked me out this week. If I was being such a grouch, he wouldn't have bothered."

"Puh-lease. Peter is so in love with you, you could ignore him, hurt his feelings, whatever, and he would still want to go out with you."

"I haven't done any of that." Madison was taken aback. Was she really coming off crabby all week?

"Fine you haven't hurt him yet, but it seems like now that you are doing more with me and planning to hang with other kids, you are a grouch."

"I'm just not used to not skating. Once I am, I'll be back to my old self."

Jordan shrugged. "We'll see. I don't think so. You're so bitter about what happened. You walk around like you've got better things to do than hang with me. How's that supposed to make me feel? You never did that before when you skated. Now you act like you're better than everyone else."

"I do not think I'm better than everyone!" Madison shouted. Now Jordan was turning her back on her, too.

"Really? I used to think that you weren't anything like Caitlin. I used to think you might be stuck up because you both skated, but when I got to know you, you proved me wrong. But this week you have the same attitude she does."

Madison crossed her arms as they walked. "I'm not like Caitlin. How could you say that?"

"I don't know. You're just walking around with an attitude."

They came to the corner where they usually parted. Madison stood still for a moment. She was waiting to see if Jordan might say more or apologize. When she didn't, Madison finally decided to break the silence. "Well I guess I'll see you around. Have fun on your date tomorrow."

"You too," Jordan said stiffly.

The girls stood in silence. Madison felt like she should apologize, but she didn't understand what she'd apologize for. Jordan waved and turned to leave; Madison let her go. In all the years they had known each other, Jordan and Madison had never fought, not even over small things. This was their first big disagreement. Madison watched Jordan walk away and loneliness swept over her. Now she would have no one to share the news of her first date with or talk to when she was sad. Madison turned sadly to walk to her own house.

She was so confused. When did life get so complicated? All of her friendships had turned into so much work. They weren't easy like they were before. Going out to perform was harder than ever. Madison hated to admit this, but she needed her mom right now. Madison wanted to be mature and handle everything on her own, but it was getting to be too much. She entered her house, relieved to be inside its safe walls. Her mother was relaxing on the couch with a cup of coffee—a rarity, Madison knew.

"Wow," Madison observed. "You're actually sitting down."

"Well you're not the only one that works hard when you're skating. I have a lot fewer clothes to wash and meals to cook and places to drive this week."

Madison hesitated slightly. "How do you like it? All the extra time, I mean?"

Mrs. Albright looked up from her magazine. "I only like it if you do. Aren't you enjoying yourself?"

Madison slid into the oversized chair, crossed her legs, and curled herself into a ball. She stared at the floor. When she looked up a few minutes later, her face was streaked with tears.

Mrs. Albright came and put her arms around Madison. "It's not so easy, quitting just like that, is it?" she stroked Madison's hair.

"No, but I don't want to go back either."

Mrs. Albright rocked on the edge of the chair. "You got burned. It was your first time, too, and the first time is always the hardest. But it doesn't have to happen again."

"But what if it does?" Madison cried. "What if it happens all over again? I couldn't handle that. It would be so embarrassing."

"How do you know that it will happen again?"

"*Because,* I couldn't explain what happened this time and sometimes I still picture myself falling. And I get nervous about everything now, so my case of nerves is getting worse, not better."

"Madison, you're getting older. Skating when you were little, you didn't even realize that people in the stands were watching you. Now you're more aware of all that and it's only natural to be more nervous."

"Liz didn't think it was okay," said Madison sadly.

"Liz didn't handle the situation very well. And I think you should talk to her about that. But you didn't handle the situation all that well, either."

"I tried..." Madison began weakly.

"You *tried* to handle everything on your own. The minute you felt different than before about performing, you should have told one of us. Pretending that everything was fine didn't work. Then it was hard for Liz to understand where you were coming from. She thought it was a freak thing, instead of an ongoing problem."

"You told me I was such a good competitor. Liz said she didn't have to worry about me. I felt pressure not to say anything. Plus, I didn't want to cause problems or look weak."

"Even the best competitors get nervous. I bet each one of them has gone through something just like you are feeling now. But you have to learn how to make your nerves help you, just like the best performers do."

"That's what Liz said. But no one is telling me *how* to do that."

Every time Madison thought of having her nerves help her skating, she got incredibly frustrated. If only someone would tell her how to control her fears instead of just telling her to fix the problem!

"I'm sure there are ways to work on it," reassured Mrs. Albright, "We can talk about them later. First, you need to make a few choices. What do you want to do about skating?"

Madison stared off into space, thinking about the impact each decision could have on her life. "I'm scared," she said finally. "I'm scared of not making my goals and then being disappointed. I don't want to quit, but I'm not ready to go back."

"If you quit, you'll never reach your goals. You have your sights set high, Maddie. If you don't make your goal, we'll deal with it, but I think you'll be more upset if you don't make the effort."

"I know," Madison sighed.

20

Date Night

Saturday morning greeted Madison with a cool November chill. Winter was in the air. It was a sudden change from the summer-like weather of the past few months. Madison's stomach flip-flopped and she wasn't sure why. She laid in bed and thought about the past week. Peter's face floated in her mind and she groaned. Now she remembered why she was dreading today: she was going to hurt Peter's feelings tonight. Madison wasn't looking forward to it. She had all day to dwell on the woeful date. She would get no sympathy from her family, either. Mrs. Albright had told Madison point blank that she had made her bed, and now she had to lie in it. She was on her own in dealing with this. That was fine by Madison, though. It was her fault that she'd agreed to go out with someone she didn't like.

Madison made herself some breakfast, then retreated to her room to study. Her class assignments had finally caught up with her. Today was the first time she had homework to do since before regionals. It was comforting to have something other than Peter on her mind. As usual, Madison used her schoolwork as a distraction, blasting through it like she always did to avoid confusing emotions. She finally forced her textbooks closed when she realized that she was halfway through the assignments due next Wednesday.

Saturdays were quiet in the Albright household. Dylan slept late, then went to work at the music store all afternoon. Dad left for work early and got home around three o'clock. Mom ran errands and did housework.

Madison had forgotten what Saturday mornings were like at home. She'd never been bored on Saturdays because her habit had been to skate all morning, study in the afternoon, and then go out with her friends at night. Her clock read twelve thirty. At least it was already afternoon. She had about six hours to get ready for her date. Madison knew some girls might take that long to choose clothes and make-up, but that wasn't Madison. She was lucky enough to have wash-and-wear hair, and she wasn't that into make-up. Besides, she didn't want to look amazing tonight. It would be wrong to lead Peter on like that. Madison thought of Jordan, who was probably in her house ransacking her closet to find the perfect outfit for Tyler.

Madison watched TV and wrote in her journal. She helped her mom unload the groceries. By five thirty, Madison decided that it was time to start getting ready to go out. She showered and washed her hair. She decided to blow dry it out—some effort to look nice was necessary. She rummaged through her wardrobe, trying to find an outfit that said we're just friends. She eventually settled on a pair of jeans with a simple blue turquoise top and a hoodie. The shiny fabric made the top a bit more feminine and flirty, but the overall look should have given off the friend vibe.

There was a knock on her door. Mrs. Albright called, "Are you getting ready?"

"Yes, I just have to dry my hair."

"Can I come in?"

Madison turned the doorknob. Mrs. Albright stepped inside. "You look nice."

"Nice, but not like I want to date him, right?" she asked nervously.

Mrs. Albright laughed. "Yes, if that's what you want to think. But it might not matter to Peter. He may still like you anyway."

"I know."

"Do you want me to finish it?" her mother offered.

"I can do it myself." Madison eyed her mom, who looked disappointed. "But you can do it if you want. I can never get it to look as good as you do."

Mrs. Albright beamed as she took the dryer from Madison. *She still likes to treat me like I'm six years old,* Madison groaned to herself. Sometimes it drove Madison crazy, but on nights like tonight it was good to have mom by her side. Mrs. Albright finished with ten minutes to spare.

Madison walked down into a kitchen full of family waiting to meet Peter. Mr. Albright sat on a stool, scowling. He didn't know that Madison had no interest in Peter. He assumed that this was the start of Madison's dating life and he wasn't the least bit pleased. Dylan was looking at a magazine and didn't even look up when Madison entered.

The doorbell rang promptly at seven and Madison moved to answer it, but Mr. Albright got there first. He opened the door to see a very nervous looking Peter.

"You must be Peter," her father boomed and stuck out his hand for Peter to shake. Peter took it nervously.

"Why don't you come in for a minute?" he pulled Peter inside the house.

"I think his mom is waiting for them, Jim. Hi, Peter." Mom to the rescue. Madison smiled her gratefulness.

"Hi, Peter. Let's go," Madison said. She waved goodbye to her parents and quickly climbed into Peter's car. The "date" had begun.

As Peter held the door open for her, Madison looked back at her house and saw her father watching from the window. He quickly pulled the drape closed when he realized Madison had spotted him. She suppressed a giggle—Dad had no idea what was going on.

"Your dad seems nice," Peter offered nervously.

"Yeah, he's sweet."

"Mom, this is Madison. Madison, this is Mom." Peter introduced.

"Nice to meet you, Madison. You look very pretty tonight." Mrs. Michaels beamed at Madison from the front seat. *Oh, no. His family is involved. I'm in so much trouble here!* Madison thought.

The car ride to the bowling alley was filled with awkward silences followed by questions about Madison and her skating. Mrs. Michaels did most of the talking. If Peter remained this silent, Madison was in for the longest night of her life. The three of them decided that two games of bowling would be enough, and Mrs. Michaels dropped them off at the alley's front door. Madison calculated that if they didn't talk much and bowled fast, this date could be over in less than an hour and a half. Peter went through the motions of proper date behavior—he held the door open, he paid, and he got her bowling shoes. It made Madison uncomfortable. The nicer Peter was, the harder it was going to be to let him down.

As they tied their bowling shoelaces, three of Peter's friends—William, Dean, and Jacob—walked in and set themselves up two alleys away. Madison was too shy to pay much attention to them. She and Peter punched their names into the scoring keypad. Madison realized that Peter had probably warned his friends to stay clear of the "couple," because Peter's friends kept to themselves

Then it was time to start the first game. "You bowl much?" she asked him.

"All the time. It's a piece of cake. Prepare to be slaughtered."

Madison nodded politely. "You first, then."

"If you insist." Peter stood looking down the lane. He prepped his ball, walked forward fast, and let it go—right into the gutter.

Madison bit her lip to keep from laughing. Peter turned around, mortified. "I'm just warming up," he said defensively. On the next shot he knocked down one pin.

"See?" he muttered, taking his seat.

Madison stood up, picked up her ball, and rolled it straight down the alley—*Strike.* She turned around and shrugged. On her next ball, she scored a nine while Peter knocked down two pins on his first roll and tossed another ball into the gutter on his second.

Unfortunately for poor Peter, the entire two games of bowling continued in much the same way. Every once in a while Madison looked over at Peter's friends, who were trying not to laugh. Their scores were much higher than Peter's. *He must be trying too hard,* she concluded.

Madison considered bowling badly on purpose, but she'd heard that guys hated to be beaten at anything by a girl, so she bowled her best. She had a better chance of breaking up with Peter if she kicked his butt.

"Wow," Peter said as they returned their bowling shoes. "Why didn't you tell me you were so good at bowling?"

"I don't usually bowl like that." Madison shrugged. As she and Peter sat down on a bench outside the bowling alley, Peter's friends walked out to their ride, still laughing as they said goodbye. She opened the box of jellies Peter had bought her.

"Want some?"

Peter took a few in his hand and sighed. "Well, I had a great time. Even if you killed me." He smiled.

Madison panicked. *What?*

"You know Maddie, I think you're really cool and I think you look really great tonight...."

Waves of tension seized Madison's body as she tried to figure out what would happen next. She wanted to scream or run away, but she was frozen on the spot. Peter was moving in closer, still complimenting her. Madison shoved the jellies into her mouth faster. Peter waited until she swallowed them. As soon as she did, he tried to kiss her. Madison flung the jellies into his lap and jumped up.

"What the—" Peter began.

"I'm sorry. Peter, I...." Madison was lost for words. She saw Mrs. Michaels' car pull into the lot. She didn't have much time. She was just going to have to say it.

"Peter I'm sorry, but I just don't like you that way. I'm not ready to be anyone's girlfriend right now. I like you as a friend, really, and I thought it would be cool to hang together tonight, but that's it." Madison half glanced at him. Shock registered on Peter's face.

Finally, he just said, "I don't know what to say." And he walked to the car where his mother waited for them and climbed in.

The ride home was silent. Peter walked her to her front door. They stood on the stoop, facing each other.

"Peter, I'm really sorry—" Madison started.

"Don't. It's okay. I shouldn't have taken so much for granted."

"No, it's my fault. I shouldn't have agreed to go out with you like this."

Peter smiled, "At least I can say that I had my first date."

Madison shrugged. "Yeah, I guess I can say that, too. I gotta go. I'll see you in school."

And with that, Peter and his mom drove away.

An Unexpected Phone Call

"Madison, phone!" Mrs. Albright shouted from downstairs. Madison ran downstairs, surprised that someone would call on a Sunday, especially on her home phone number. "Who is it?" she mouthed to her mom.

"It's Liz," she said.

Madison felt a lump rise to her throat. She really hadn't decided whether to quit. She shook her head, but Mrs. Albright firmly handed her the phone, saying, "It's time."

Madison reluctantly took the handset and tried to collect herself. "Hi, Liz."

"Madison, how have you been?" Liz asked in a sweet tone.

"Oh, fine," Madison was guarded. She didn't feel comfortable sharing her recent ups and downs with Liz.

"Enjoying your week of freedom?"

"Yes, I'm thinking about making it permanent," Madison blurted out. It wasn't what she'd intended to say, but somehow the words slipped out.

"Oh?" Madison could picture the frown on Liz's face. "It's up to you of course, but regionals was a pretty bad way to end your competitive career."

"Maybe, but something about skating doesn't feel right."

Liz started, "I have a few reasons for calling you. The first was to apologize for the way I reacted to your skate in Minnesota. I should have been more understanding and open to listening to you. I was just so shocked. A case of nerves like that has never gotten to me, so I didn't get what you were going through."

"You had a right to be upset. I let you down," Madison said.

"Of course I was disappointed. But I should have made it clear that I was disappointed with what happened and not with you as a person. I saw how hurt you were by the things I said and I'm sorry."

Madison took a deep breath. "I'm sorry, too. For not telling you what was going on, I mean. I just didn't want you to lose confidence in me."

Madison could "see" Liz nod at her end of the line.

"I still do have faith in you, Maddie. I got a call yesterday from USFS. The girl who placed fourth at regionals—you remember her? You knew she was injured, right? Well, she can't skate at Junior Nationals. Since you placed fifth, you are the first alternate."

Madison could not believe what she was hearing. Just when she was ready to give up skating entirely, a wonderful opportunity presented itself. She needed Liz to tell her it was true. "So I can compete at Junior Nationals?"

"Yes. You have to agree to go by tomorrow afternoon or the spot goes to the sixth-place finisher. The competition is in a month."

"Wow." Madison was stunned.

"So are you going?"

"I don't know," Madison answered. "I'm not sure if I want to. It's too painful to go back out there. And what if I get this spot and then I blow it at nationals, too?"

"You can't think like that. You deserve this spot. We're definitely going to have to work on your mindset, but I think you can pull it off."

"When is the exact deadline tomorrow?"

"Noon, but honestly, I'd rather not push the decision to the last minute. I don't want the officials to think you're not interested and go with the other girl without a reply from you."

"Can I call you back?" Madison asked.

Liz sighed. "Yes, but make it today. I want an answer today."

"Okay."

"Can you put your mother on the phone, please?"

Madison handed the phone over to her mother and retreated to her bedroom. Her mother talked quietly with Liz for what must have been half an hour. Madison was afraid to admit how overjoyed she was at the idea of competing at Junior Nationals. She could still manage to accomplish her goal, and regionals would be remembered as just a minor bump in the road.

Over the past week Madison had really grown to understand just how big a part of her life skating was and how much she missed being at the rink. But Madison was afraid, too—afraid that it wouldn't be the same when she went back to train. She could never again look at the sport without knowing that it had scarred her. Even if she came back from that, would she love the sport as much? Would she drive herself to train as hard as she did before? Madison worried about messing up at competition again. At Junior Nationals, everyone would know that she came as the alternate. If she skated poorly, it would look like she didn't deserve to be there.

Deep down, Madison wanted to prove to herself and everyone that she was capable of performing an amazing routine. Committing to it, no matter what the outcome, was what prevented Madison from agreeing to return to skating right away.

Madison waited in her room for an hour after Mrs. Albright hung up from talking to Liz, but her mother didn't come in to talk. This decision was entirely up to Madison. Her mom had said her piece before, and now Madison had to choose what to do. Her head told her that she didn't need the stress that skating brought, that it was too expensive, and that she was taking a big risk by trying to redeem herself. Her heart told her that she loved skating and that there was nothing she'd rather do than accomplish her skating dreams. She remembered the feeling of gliding powerfully across the ice and how good it felt to skate a clean routine.

Several agonizing hours later, Madison picked up the phone.

"Hello?" answered Liz.

"I want to do it," Madison said with determination.

"Good. I'm proud of you, Maddie. And I promise to be there to help you through it this time. We have a month. Come to the rink tomorrow afternoon and we'll get started."

"I'll be there."

"Welcome back! See you tomorrow."

"Bye." Madison turned to find her mother standing in the archway between the kitchen and family room.

"What did you decide?" she asked.

"I decided to try. I start tomorrow."

Mrs. Albright rushed over and gave Madison a hug. "Honey, I'm so happy for you. I knew you wouldn't quit."

"How?"

"I know you. You like to finish what you start. Besides, you weren't ready *not* to skate. Look at how you handled this past week."

Madison thought back through the week's events. She had been unpleasant to be around. Jordan still wasn't talking to her; neither was Dylan. And after last night, Peter wouldn't be either.

Madison giggled. "Yeah, most people I know hate me right now."

"They'll get over it. You'll be back to yourself in no time. Are you skating in the morning or afternoon?"

"Afternoon."

"I'll call the school and tell the office we're back on the normal schedule."

"Sounds good." Madison returned to her room, trying to grasp what had just happened. She had been secretly wishing for this all week. Being able to skate at Junior Nationals gave Madison a fantastic new goal. It might be easier to get over her nerves if she put a time limit on the recovery process. Just thinking about Junior Nationals set the butterflies aflutter in her stomach. At the moment, they were "bugging" her the right way. She was looking forward to getting back on the ice. She had a month to prepare. Madison knew her skills would be ready by December, but she couldn't guarantee a sharp mental edge. She hated to admit when she was wrong, but as soon as she'd hung up with Liz, Madison knew that to win she would have to train differently. She would have to voice her concerns and work on visualizing clean programs, even if she had to picture each jump a thousand times before she finally saw herself land one.

A couple of hours later, a calm fell over Madison, knowing that she would be going back to her old routine tomorrow. Mom was right. The past week had given Madison too much time to think. She needed to be busy in order to stay focused but relaxed.

That night at dinner, Madison decided to announce the news to her family. She waited until everyone was seated and she could command their full attention.

She cleared her throat. "I have something to say." Her parents looked up, but Dylan kept his eyes on his plate and continued to eat. Madison ignored him. She would have his attention soon enough.

"Liz called today." That did it. Dylan's head snapped up.

"Did you quit?" he asked, parroting her sometimes-whiny voice.

Madison made a face. "She called me to see whether I wanted to go to Junior Nationals." She waited for a reaction. Both Dylan and her father looked confused. Madison went on to explain how the fourth-place regionals competitor had withdrawn.

Mr. Albright sighed. "I'm so glad you decided to skate. And it's great that you get to go."

"Yeah," Dylan agreed. "Now you can make up for regionals."

Madison's face fell. "I'm trying to forget about that," she spat.

"Shush, Dylan," Mrs. Albright scolded. "Let's just be happy for Madison tonight. This is great news!"

"Just as long as we get a puppy this time," Dylan mumbled so only Madison could hear. She scowled at him. Why was he making such stupid comments? He was the one that was so insistent that she keep skating in the first place! Madison's anger swelled up. Luckily, the conversation turned to the usual Sunday night scheduling session, and skating at nationals was dropped for the evening.

As Madison went to bed, she felt less excited than she had at first. Her reservations were coming back as strong as before. *Why are they starting so soon?* she wondered. The pressure to make up for her poor skate at regionals came crashing down on her: *Am I really good enough to win against the regional champions at Junior Nationals?*

147

22

Red Flag

Monday morning, Madison felt supercharged with energy. She had an extra spring in her step as she walked into school. Training would be intense for the next few weeks, but she didn't care. She was happy to have her old routine back.

When Madison stowed her backpack in her locker, she grew worried. Jordan was nowhere near where they usually met in the morning. Shouldn't Jordan be over their fight by now? It had only been two days, but Madison already missed Jordan's company. She spotted Jordan's blonde ponytail in the front row in homeroom. Jordan turned around and waved at Madison. Madison grinned and mouthed "Hi" before standing for the pledge.

After the announcements, Peter tapped her shoulder.

"Just friends, then, Maddie," he whispered, leaning over her.

"Yes," she replied, hesitating, but then seeing the hurt in his eyes. Her good mood fell several notches, and her eyes got a little watery. Then a shadow crossed her desk. Jordan stood in front of her as Peter walked away quickly.

"Hi," Madison said, relieved to talk to her friend again.

"How was your weekend?" Jordan asked tentatively. Neither girl was sure who was mad at whom.

"Don't ask," Madison laughed. "No, not all of it was bad. Liz called. I get to fill in at Junior Nationals."

Jordan's eyebrows shot up. "Like, you're competing there? So you have to skate again?"

"Yes."

149

Jordan let out an excited "Yes!" and the whole class turned to stare at her.

"What are you looking at?" she taunted, and they quickly went back to their business. "I'm so happy for you, Maddie!"

"So is everyone. I guess I *was* crabby last week. I probably deserved you yelling at me."

Jordan looked at the floor. "I'm sorry about that. You were so upset and I didn't know how to help you. It frustrated me, so I just wanted you to get over it so you could be happy again."

"Well I am. I start training today."

"And Caitlin can't go to this competition, right?" Jordan asked, wearing a wicked smile.

"No."

"That makes it even better. You are gonna have your run of the school when this is over and you're the champ."

"Whoa! No pressure, okay? I want to keep this low key."

Jordan nodded slowly. She could never understand why Madison didn't want her skating accomplishments blasted around school. Jordan reveled in attention, but being noticed and constant scrutiny made Madison want to jump out of her skin.

"You got it," said Jordan in her *if it were me, I'd…*tone.

***

Mrs. Albright pulled up promptly at one o'clock. She was smiling too, happy to have her daughter in a good mood again. She was glad to hear that Madison and Jordan made up, although she'd never doubted they would.

Soon the car pulled up to the Arctic Circle Ice Arena. Madison lingered a few moments in the car. As excited as she was, she still felt some anxiety about heading into the rink today.

"Madison, there's a line of cars forming behind us. You have to get out now."

"Okay," sighed Madison. She took her bag.

"I'll pick you up at the usual time. And remember, today is only the first day back. If things aren't great today, don't worry," Mrs. Albright said reassuring her and drove off.

Thousands of worries still floated in Madison's head. She walked through the lobby and into the cool arena, checking out the scene. Liz was already teaching. Four skaters were practicing. The rink was quieter than usual: *What a relief!* Madison thought. During the weeks following regionals, lots of skaters took time off. Some quit or switched coaches. It was a time to start over. Madison liked the vibe in the arena, but by the time she stepped onto the ice, her stomach was full of butterflies. *Breathe, breathe,* Madison told herself.

"Hi, Maddie." Liz skated up to her and gave her a hug.

"How are you?"

"I'm good. Ready to get to work?" Liz asked matter of factly. She wasn't one to waste time with sappy reunions.

"I think so," replied Madison timidly.

"I need to hear more conviction. Say you're ready like you mean it."

"I'm ready." Madison tried to sound more forceful.

Liz made a face. "Better, but still not convincing. Go warm up. I'll be with you in a minute."

Madison skated away. She felt a little off balance because of her week off. Madison wobbled through backward and forward crossovers as well as the edges and turns she did to get her balance back.

A few minutes later Liz returned. "Okay. Warm up your jumps. I want to start with those."

Madison felt tension rise as she prepared to take off for her first few jumps. Today she was determined to meet the emotion head on. She forced herself to think only of the few technical tips Liz told her about each jump. She was landing jumps much easier today than at the competition. She skated back to Liz and stood before her proudly.

Instead of the expected praise, Liz simply said, "Too bad you couldn't do that at regionals. All right, I want to run a section of your short—the one with the triple toe. No music. Do the jump no matter what."

Madison nodded. The way Liz said that last sentence made her wary. She had a feeling something was going to be different about this section. Madison started to skate, marking the landing of the double axel and then proceeding into the footwork that led up to her triple toe. Madison was still skating rougher than usual, but she attacked the section to the best of her ability. She rounded the corner and stepped forward to set up for her jump. From out of nowhere, a huge red towel flew across Madison's face. She blinked and practically tripped over her own feet.

"Jump!" Liz yelled. Madison vaulted herself into the air. She wasn't surprised when she found herself splattered across the ice a second later. She hadn't been focused when she took off. Madison looked around, dazed.

"Get up," Liz ordered. Madison dusted the snow off her clothes and skated over to Liz.

"What—" Madison stopped as she saw the red towel in Liz's hand. She grew angry. "What did you do that for? I could have been hurt!"

"It's an exercise in concentration," said Liz, dismissing Madison's concern. "What did you feel when you saw the towel in front of you?"

"Totally freaked out!" said Madison, still spooked.

"Like you did at competition?"

Madison thought for a moment. Yes, she had just experienced feelings similar to those she had at regionals. This made her even angrier. Liz had totally tricked her. She looked at Liz. "I guess so," she said reluctantly, unwilling to give in.

Liz smirked in satisfaction. "An athlete in complete control of her mind and emotions would have landed that jump without batting an eye. You have to be so in the moment that nothing will faze you. Try it again."

Madison sucked in a breath and skated away. This time she would be prepared for the towel. She was sure she would land her jump. She rounded the corner once more. In the middle of one of her three turns, she saw the red towel fly across her face. Madison lost her balance and tripped. She had to put her hand on the ice to keep from falling.

"Jump!" Liz commanded. Madison hurried to get her rhythm back to try her triple toe. She landed better than before, but she still fell. Madison got up and kicked the ice with her toepick.

"None of that," Liz said. "Again."

Madison bit her lip to hold her tongue. Liz was just doing her job, even if she was being harsh.

For the next hour, Liz made Madison skate sections of her program over and over again. Each time she waved the towel in front of Madison's face at a different time and spot. Madison fell and fell. She landed just one jump that whole hour. The more times she fell, the more upset she got. Madison came to realize that she didn't have to be in the competitive arena to feel the same emotions she had at regionals.

Once the hour was up, Liz called Madison over. "That was good today."

"You're killing me!" Madison said.

"I know, but it's not technique you need to work on. It's learning to not get distracted and dealing with your nerves that are the problem."

"Yeah, and they're still a problem. I didn't land any jumps!"

Liz put an arm around her. "You'll get it. You don't have a long time to master it, but you will. Even if you don't skate clean at nationals you'll be okay, as long as you skate better than last time and prove to yourself that you can do it."

Madison nodded. She needed to give herself a break; it was only her first day back.

"We'll be doing that exercise and others like it everyday until nationals." Liz explained.

"Okay."

"Go home. Rest. You need to take really good care of yourself this month. If you feel sick, stay home from school. Eat healthy. Go to bed on time. You know the drill."

Again, Madison just nodded. She got the same instructions before every competition. In the locker room, she plopped onto a bench, exhausted. Madison closed her eyes. She could fall asleep right here and now.

"Back at the rink? I didn't think you'd want to show your face after regionals." Caitlin's cold voice brought Madison out of her stupor.

"At least I'm going to Junior Nationals."

"By default," Caitlin sneered. "You're not going because you deserve it. You're going because they need a substitute."

"Caitlin, I'm tired. I've had a hard enough time as it is. Can't you just leave me alone?"

"You just can't handle the truth," Caitlin sneered again.

"I can take the truth. The truth is I screwed up, but I have a chance to make up for it and I'm going to take it."

"Well, just know that even if you do great at Junior Nationals, it was luck and not your talent that got you there."

"Deal with your own life and stay out of mine." Madison pushed past her and went outside to wait for her mother. Rather than break into tears like she had the week before regionals, Madison laughed to herself about this conversation: *I finally did it! I finally stood up to Caitlin!* Mrs. Albright's car pulled up. Madison beamed as she climbed in.

"Good day?" Mrs. Albright asked.

"You could say that," Madison nodded. It was a good day. She had taken steps to change how she reacted to competition and she'd put Caitlin in her place. Madison could feel herself becoming more confident already. She didn't anticipate having problems with Caitlin anymore.

23

Newfound Confidence

BAM! Madison fell on her hip with a thud. A week and a half had passed and she had made little progress with her concentration exercises. She was still falling on her jumps way more often than she was landing them. Time was ticking and Madison was starting to panic. She had barely done any full run-throughs of her programs and when she did, a towel or soaker was always being thrown in front of her or a loud noise sounded before she jumped. She had yet to do a clean program.

Madison tried to stay motivated, but her concentration was slipping. Who wanted to get on the ice and fall hundreds of times a day? Nevertheless, Madison put on a brave face for her mother, for herself, and everyone else. She wanted to skate. It was her choice to continue and that meant that she had to accept everything that came with skating again. She grew antsy, thinking, *Junior Nationals are in two weeks and I'm nowhere near ready.* On Thursday, with two weeks to go till the competition, Liz came to practice without any props.

"Let's do a normal run-through today," she said.

Madison was so relieved she wanted to hug Liz. Instead, she shrugged and said, "Sure."

Madison took her position to run her long. She assumed that this program would go smoothly. There were no distractions. She took off for her double axel and—boom!—landed it. With a sigh of relief, Madison prepared for the next element in her program. She catapulted herself into the air and turned the two and a half revolutions required for a triple toe. She landed it flawlessly. Grinning, she realized that the prior week's training had prepared her well. She was on cloud nine as she completed her program. The lightness in her heart translated into quickness in her feet, and faster spins than ever. Her skating had a joy to it that she had not experienced in a very long time.

Finally, it came time for the final jump in her program. Madison was confident that she would nail it. She turned to step forward and suddenly a burst of red flashed in front of her face. Startled, Madison felt herself start to lose her footing. *No!* she commanded. *No, pull yourself together. You can do this!* She threw herself into the air and came down on one foot in a perfect landing position. Liz cheered as Madison entered her last combination spin. Madison pulled her arms high above her head in a back scratch position and jumped out of the spin and into her final pose. She waited the customary five seconds while her imaginary crowd clapped. Madison clasped her hands together and let out a whoop.

She skated over to Liz. "Did you see that?" Madison panted, still out of breath from both skating hard and a rush of happiness.

Liz smiled and patted her on the back. "I'm very proud of you. You had no idea that last test was coming and you handled it beautifully. What were you thinking?"

"I don't know," Madison responded, but then added, "No. I know exactly what I was thinking. I decided that I was going to land the jump and that was that. I just made up my mind to not let the towel affect me."

Liz nodded. "Good. You're getting stronger mentally. Can you train yourself to think like that all the time?"

"I can try. It sure would be great to be that focused. It'd be impossible to get too anxious then."

"That was my point, Maddie."

"I didn't really get why you did all that crazy stuff, but I guess it's paying off." Madison was jubilant. For the first time in weeks, she believed that she was capable of showing everyone what she could do.

Liz shrugged. "Don't get too excited. I still have one more challenge to see how focused you really are."

Madison's heart sank. She hoped this test wouldn't mess with her new level of confidence. "Tomorrow?" she asked half-heartedly.

"No, you deserve a break. Sometime next week. Tomorrow will just be a normal practice."

"Good." Madison stepped off the ice still glowing, thinking, *I skated my first clean program since regionals. Everything is finally coming together.* Now all she had to do was keep it together through the competition.

***

Saturday afternoon Madison finished the week's skating practice. She had only four days on the ice left before she headed to Washington, D.C. Friday's practice had been just acceptable—not as good as Thursday's. Liz assured her that it was normal for an athlete to be a little off her game a few days prior to her event.

Madison was looking forward to a relaxing weekend. She decided to see Jordan tonight. Staying home to rest before regionals had left her feeling nervous and tired. Now she'd change her approach.

Jordan's mom picked her up at seven. The girls were heading to the movies.

"So, Madison I hear you're going to Washington next Thursday," said Jordan's mom, Mrs. Riley.

"Yes, to compete at Junior Nationals."

"You must be so excited. Are you nervous? I would get so nervous I would trip all over the place," Jordan's mother continued. The girls exchanged glances. In the past, even talking about a competition with anyone would shoot shivers of terror down Madison's back.

Madison tossed her hair. "I'm a little nervous," she admitted, "but not nearly as much as usual. I've been working really hard on not letting it get to me."

"I guess you get used to it after you do it so many times."

"That's what I'm counting on," she said under her breath. Jordan giggled. Madison turned her attention back to Jordan's mother.

"Yes, I think you do get used to it," Mrs. Riley replied, pulling up to the movie theatre. "Have fun. I'll be back when it's over."

Madison and Jordan thanked her and walked inside.

"Tyler!" Jordan squealed and she raced over to give him a hug. Madison only smiled. She was used to having boys occasionally show up on one of their movie nights. It never bothered Madison. Tyler would just sit with them.

"Maddie, look who's here," said Jordan, dragging Tyler over to her.

"Hi," Madison said. Tyler nodded in response. They loaded up on popcorn, ushered themselves into the theatre, and took their seats. Madison was pushed to the end of the row while Jordan and Tyler huddled close together. They had picked out a comedy, and it paid off. It was hysterical. Madison sat through the entire movie laughing out loud without thinking about Junior Nationals. When the lights came on, the moviegoers smiled at each other as they dusted themselves clean of popcorn. Then Jordan and Tyler said their good-byes, and the girls walked out to Mrs. Riley's car while Jordan gushed about how much she liked Tyler. Then Jordan switched to talk of how great the movie was.

When she got home, Madison went straight upstairs. She wanted to go to sleep right away. She either wanted to be busy or sleeping this entire weekend. That way her mind would not dwell on thoughts of nationals.

24

One Last Test

On Wednesday, one day before leaving for nationals, Madison felt especially anxious. As she got on the ice to practice, she still hadn't had the last test Liz had promised and Madison couldn't guess what to expect. Then she got her surprise. The ice rink was empty—no skaters on the ice, no parents in the stands. Something really strange was going on.

Liz called, "We're doing a mock competition today. Go in the locker room for ten minutes and then come back out here."

Madison nodded and got off the ice. All the thoughts and feelings she had at regionals came flooding back. This was truly going to test how much progress she had made.

"All right, come out." Liz opened the door, and Madison observed the scene. The only difference was that the stands were filled with coaches, skaters, and families. Madison spotted her mom and her heart sank. Liz was really trying to freak her out!

Liz instructed her, "Okay, you get a five minute warm-up and then do your short."

She walked around to the sound system, then boomed, "Will the next skater please take the ice for her five minute warm-up?"

Madison shot out of the door like a rocket and started to warm up, looking up at the stands as she stroked. Liz had gotten some of the coaches to sit where the judges would. The other skaters and parents cheered as she passed. The butterflies were fluttering in Madison's stomach. She got through her spins without too much tension and moved onto warming up her jumps.

"One minute remaining in the warm-up," Liz said over the speaker. The entire warm-up went well. *It's the actual event that's the problem,* Madison fretted silently.

"This concludes the warm-up. Please clear the ice." Madison got off and removed her sweater. Her hands were clammy and her heart was racing, but she was relatively calm.

"Representing the Arctic Circle Figure Skating Club, please give a warm welcome to Madison Albright!"

Madison skated to the center of the ice to the sound of polite applause. The music started and Madison's breath caught in her chest. She wanted to run and hide, but there was no way out. Her body was already moving through muscle memory. Pacing herself, she prepared for her first jump. To her immense surprise, she landed it with no problem. Madison's confidence soared and she took off through the rest of the program like it was a walk in the park. She finished to rousing applause from the stands. Her mom gave her a standing ovation. Madison's heart skipped a beat—in a good way—as she skated over to Liz.

"I did it!" she breathed.

"Yes, you did. Do you think you can repeat this in Washington?"

"I think so. Almost everything was the same as at regionals. But I held myself together today."

Liz nodded. "Yes, you did. Tomorrow I want you to just run your programs and then we leave."

Mrs. Albright had been working tirelessly to secure two inexpensive tickets to Washington, D.C., which Madison reported to Liz. "We leave tomorrow night, after school and practice."

She got off the ice and cooled down while Mrs. Albright pulled the car up.

"That was great today, honey. You didn't seem nervous," her mom said proudly.

"Oh, I was," Madison laughed. 'I just knew how to control it better this time."

One Last Test

"I'm glad. That's not an easy thing to overcome."
"Well I just hope it lasts. I only have a few day to get through and then I can let down."
"Yes," Mrs. Albright agreed. "And you can take a much needed rest."
"Who said anything about resting?" Madison laughed. "I have to get started on next season."
By the time they got back home again, the light was already starting to fade. "Go pack. I want you in bed early tonight. I'll make dinner," her mother ordered.
Madison got her suitcase out and packed her best jeans and sweaters. She moved onto her skating dresses next. Her fingers lingered on her lucky pink practice dress. It wasn't really nice enough for competition, but Madison packed it anyway. Maybe she wasn't as nervous as before, but she wasn't completely cured. A few superstitions never hurt anyone.
Madison just finished packing as her mom called that dinner was ready. Dylan was working late, so it was just Madison and her parents. Her dad lifted a glass.
"I want to toast Madison and all the hard work she's done these past few weeks. Mom and I support you no matter what happens. We love you and we want you to be happy. I'm sure you'll do fine, but if the results aren't perfect, just know it's okay and we're here for you."
They clanked their juice glasses, then Madison put her head in her hands. Her dad could be so cheesy sometimes, but she appreciated his support. "Thanks Dad. And who knows, maybe we'll get a puppy soon."
Mr. Albright firmly shook his head. "I don't want you to worry about that. The result doesn't matter. Even if you skate well and don't place, we can talk about getting the dog."
"I told you I don't want it like that." Madison dug her heels in.
"Okay, you two," Mrs. Albright warned. "You're both too stubborn. Worry about the dog later. Madison, is everything settled with your teachers?"
"Yes. They were not happy about it. They complained that I had just recently missed school and blah, blah, blah."

161

"But it worked out?"

"Yes, I got all my assignments ahead of time. I actually have to do them while we're in Washington, though."

The garage door opened and Dylan walked in.

"I didn't even hear any music from down the street," Mr. Albright said approvingly.

"I turned it down when I got to the house." Dylan said, turning to Madison. "You ready to go tomorrow?"

"Yes."

"Good." Dylan walked out of the room. Madison turned to look at her parents.

"What's with him?"

"He wants you to do well," Mrs. Albright said.

"Couldn't he just say that?" Madison asked.

"Sometimes that's hard for guys," Mrs. Albright said.

"Whatever," said Madison using her catchphrase anytime Dylan did something she didn't understand.

"Go get ready for bed." Mrs. Albright shooed her out of the kitchen.

Back up in her bedroom, Madison glanced at the packed bags. They were all ready to go. Was she? She still had nerves, but she was dealing with them. She would take whatever came with grace and acceptance. Climbing into bed for the night, she visualized the next few days: Getting on the plane; arriving at the rink; skating in qualifying, short, and long; and stepping on top of the podium. Not once did she visualize herself falling. That was the very best part.

25

Taking Off

Madison awoke to the buzz of her alarm clock and glanced out the window. There was a light blanket of snow on the ground— the first snow of the year.

Madison made herself a quick breakfast. Mom would drive Madison to school, but Mr. Albright and Dylan had gotten up to wish Madison good luck.

Madison loaded the car and turned to say goodbye to everyone. She hugged her dad and then turned to Dylan as her parents hugged and kissed goodbye. He swooped her up into a big hug. "You'll be good. I know you can do this."

"Thanks, Dylan. Why are you being so nice?" Madison asked.

"Because I want you to do great. And I think you can. *And* I know you love it."

Madison hugged Dylan. " I do. Thanks, I guess."

He ruffled her hair. "Yeah, just make me proud."

"I'll do my best."

Madison ran to the car and hopped inside. She was still puzzled by Dylan's sudden kindness and support, but she did appreciate them.

Mrs. Albright dropped her off at school. Madison was only going to attend half a day so that she could skate and still make the flight to Washington.

Madison sat through homeroom, letting her mind wander to the competition. No announcement about Junior Nationals was made, so no one asked Madison where she was going or wished her good luck. She felt a twinge of regret, missing people's good luck wishes. After three more classes, it was time to head to her locker and pack up; Jordan was there to send her off. Her friend watched as Madison collected her books from the shelf.

"This is so exciting. You have to go sightseeing while you're there," Jordan said.

"I should. I will if I have time." Madison agreed. She slammed her locker shut.

"I'll walk you to the door."

As the girls walked down the hall, Peter walked toward them, talking to a friend. He just glimpsed Madison as he passed. He slowed a moment and waved. Madison felt relieved. Peter looked happy. *He's over it,* she thought.

At the entrance of the school, they saw Mrs. Albright already waiting outside. Jordan threw her arms around Madison. "Good luck! It's gonna be great!" she reassured her. Madison nodded and smiled at Jordan. They waved goodbye as Madison got into the car.

Upon arriving at the rink, she hurried into the locker room to get changed. Madison had only forty minutes to skate before they drove to the airport. Madison quickly skated onto the ice and began warming up. A good half hour into her practice she saw Liz get on the ice with another student. The girl turned to face her—Caitlin. *She just can't give me any peace can she? What does she really think her being here will do?* Madison finished her practice without so much as glancing at Caitlin. Caitlin was trying to constantly get Madison's attention. She uttered mean remarks under her breath and tried to psych her out each time she went into a jump. The only person Madison watched was Liz to see if she saw what Caitlin was up to. Liz was frowning, but Madison wasn't sure if it was Caitlin's skating or her behavior that displeased Liz.

"Good job, Maddie," Liz mumbled as Madison finished. "I'll call you tonight." Caitlin skated over and shot Madison a dirty look. Madison only smiled in response. Caitlin's frown hardened.

Madison got off the ice feeling pretty good about herself and her skating. If the last practice was any indicator, Madison concluded that she was in good shape.

She met her mom at the door. In a short time they would be at the airport and then on their way. Madison's stomach flip-flopped. Suddenly, the competition became more real. The time had come. She was actually going!

***

"How was the flight?" Liz asked over the phone. Madison was lying on the bed in her hotel room.

"Good. Bumpy at the end though. And you can't get out of your seat once you fly into Washington. If you do, the plane has to make an emergency landing for security."

"Wow, I'll remember that. Everything else okay? The hotel is fine? You are fine?" Liz asked in a soothing tone.

"Yes," Madison replied confidently. She really did feel pretty good. She'd only had one small freakout on the plane. Madison hated to fly, and she cursed the day she started figure skating when the plane hit a patch of turbulence.

"Good." Liz didn't sound skeptical this time. "All right. Take care of yourself. You know the drill. I will see you tomorrow."

They said good night and Madison lay back in bed. This felt so different from regionals. She was actually excited to practice tomorrow. Mrs. Albright came and sat on the edge of the bed. "How are you doing?"

Madison shrugged. "Fine. I'm not nervous at all."

Her mother watched her and Madison blushed. "Okay, maybe a little, but I'm trying not to think about it."

"Oh no, I'm not letting you get out of talking about it this time. That's what got you into trouble. Whatever you're feeling, you gotta spill."

Madison sighed. She thought for a moment about what to say. It was hard to clearly define what was making her apprehensive. Mrs. Albright waited patiently until Madison finally explained that it was fear of repeating regionals that bothered her. She opened up to her mother and mentioned a few other issues, too. Just talking about them made her feel better.

Mrs. Albright gave Madison words of encouragement and assurance, which were what she really needed. She concluded, "Just remember what your dad said. We love you and we're proud of you no matter what. There's no pressure from us."

"I know. Thanks."

Mrs. Albright kissed Madison on the forehead and turned out the light. In just a few short hours, the competition would be underway.

26

Nervous Again?

Madison was a basket of nerves at the gate, waiting for practice to begin. She wore her lucky pink practice dress and she was fidgeting with her hair.

Liz took her hand and said, "Stop picking. It makes you look nervous."

"I am nervous." Madison said.

Liz arched an eyebrow. "I thought we were over this."

"So did I, but this morning all the nerves came flooding back."

The announcer called the skaters' names and Madison reluctantly stepped on the ice. Her legs felt weak and her arms were heavy. She did her best to showcase her speed as she warmed up. The other skaters were really no better than the competitors had been at regionals. Madison knew she could beat everyone if she stayed focused. She continued to practice as the announcer called out a skater's name and played her music. Madison was fifth to practice to her music. She'd had half the practice session to make herself even more nervous and anticipate skating her short. When the announcer finally called her name, Madison was shaking. She started her program with a rocky entrance to a spin and it went downhill from there. The only jump she landed was her triple toe. Tears formed in her eyes as she skated over to Liz. Liz did not look pleased.

"What happened?" she demanded.

Madison lowered her eyes. "I got nervous. I didn't want to make a mistake. I think that made me tense up."

Liz pursed her lips. "You can't skate expecting to make mistakes, Maddie. You have to be in the moment and think of each element as it comes."

"I know, I know!" Madison snapped. "I can do it in practice, I just can't do it here."

Liz gave her a long, hard look. "Yes you can. You just have to make up your mind to do it."

"It was easier when you were flapping that towel in my face," Madison scowled.

"Let's get through the rest of the practice. We'll talk about the rest later."

Madison had a shaky practice the rest of the time, although every element improved after her run-through. By the time she returned to her hotel room, she was completely dejected.

Mrs. Albright did her best to calm her down.

"Let's talk about this," Mrs. Albright said soothingly. "Go through everything you felt and we'll see when you started to lose your confidence."

Madison thought hard through the day's events. She'd been nervous the minute she woke up. She felt like she was walking through a fog. Everything she did had an extra air of tension. Still, Madison was unsure why she felt the way she did. The anxiousness just came on suddenly and left just as quickly. She explained this to her mom in great detail as Mrs. Albright listened intently.

"Sounds to me like being in the actual arena is what gets you. Try to remember what you thought about and how you felt during the mock competition."

"I tried. But I don't really remember what I thought about that day. I was so relaxed, everything just came naturally."

"So, let it come naturally. Don't think so much. Let it all flow." Mrs. Albright suggested.

Madison shrugged. "I can try. But I don't think it's so simple to just relax."

Mrs. Albright agreed. She had done homework on her own in the weeks before the competition, studying some techniques that could help if Maddie started to lose focus. Now was the time to try some of her newfound techniques. She explained how to do deep breathing and how to tense and then relax her muscles in order to let the tension she felt flow out of her body. Madison tried the exercises a few times. She found herself relaxing on the spot.

"Run through these breathing routines a series of times tomorrow morning before you compete. You can even do it standing at the door. And remember, even when you're skating, you can always find places to take deep breaths in your routine."

Madison tried the exercises a few more times, while her mom watched and made suggestions. Madison could feel the improvements in her breathing and relaxation. They were still not enough. She hoped that she could master how to relax by Sunday.

***

"Madison," Mrs. Albright shook her gently awake. "You have to get up now."

"Why?" Madison said groggily.

"Because you have to compete today, remember?" Mrs. Albright smiled.

"Oh, yeah." She got up slowly and stretched. She had slept well—no bad dreams, no pictures in her head of falling. She bounded to the bathroom.

Mrs. Albright looked surprised. "You're in a good mood. And just think, qualifying is already over and you did well. After today you'll be more than halfway through," she observed.

"Yeah, I feel ready," Madison said confidently.

"You do?"

"Yes I have the exercises you gave me and I've made up my mind that I can do this and I won't let being in the arena bother me."

"I'm so glad you feel that way."

They got skates and bags ready, adding the treat of getting a room-service breakfast delivered, and forty-five minutes later the duo headed to the competition arena. The butterflies were going strong in Madison's stomach, but she refused to let them take over. Her stomach twanged as she entered the

169

rink and stored her bag in the locker room. Warming up off-ice was the challenging part. Madison walked through her routine and had momentary flashes of falling, but she took a few deep breaths and quickly turned her thoughts around.

Liz came up behind her. "How are you?" she wore a worried look.

"I'm good," Madison reported firmly. "Really." She added the assurance because Liz looked unconvinced.

"Okay, I am tense. But I can handle this. I have a few tricks up my sleeve."

"Oh?"

"My mom showed them to me. They helped me relax."

"Well let's just hope they work," Liz said shortly. She was in full-blown competition mode. She was all business and snapping as usual. It wasn't the most supportive of answers but Madison decided to accept it. She wasn't going to get anything better out of Liz.

Liz checked her watch. "You'd better go get changed. You skate third. I want you at the door five minutes before your group is called."

Madison hurried off to get dressed. Madison pulled her blue tie-dyed dress out of the costume bag and carefully put it on. She inspected her reflection in the mirror and decided she looked appropriate. She zipped up her warm-up jacket and headed into the cold arena. She recognized some of the skaters from the regional championships, but most were from other regions and were new faces. For some reason, Madison found being at nationals more relaxing than any other competition she'd ever attended. She felt a greater responsibility to deliver a good performance, but it just seemed like she would do what she needed to and that was it.

"Will the next group of skaters please take the ice for their five minute warm-up?"

The announcement startled Madison. She was deep into her relaxation exercises. Usually Liz would be buzzing around her giving her last-minute advice. Today she stood silently beside her and let Madison take control of what she needed to do.

Madison stepped onto the ice to the applause of the crowd.

She looked up into the stands determined to view the audience as a support system and not an intimidating group waiting to judge her. She warmed up with other skaters, comparing her speed and presentation to theirs. Today she was much faster and polished than the rest. Pleased with herself, Madison skated without so much as a tiny stumble.

Soon the announcer was calling time and the girls cleared the ice. Madison got off and shook her legs out as the first competitor was announced. Liz and Madison went into the warm hallway to prepare. Liz was watching her intently.

"I feel like a bad coach for not saying anything to you."

Madison smiled and laughed, "No, you're a good coach because you know that you need to let me do what I had to do to get ready."

Liz nodded in silence. Madison tensed and relaxed her muscles. She rolled her neck and tried to center herself. She tried to block out all outside thoughts. All she focused on was her technique and the tasks she needed to perform.

"Maddie, come on. Let's stand by the door. You're after Jamie."

Madison walked to the gate and unzipped her jacket, placing it around her shoulders to keep warm. She turned her back to the ice and left her earbuds in. That way she could not hear the audience's reaction to Jamie's performance. Soon Liz tapped her on the shoulder and she took her jacket off. She stepped onto the ice and faced Liz. Her stomach was flip-flopping and hands tingling as she tried to get comfortable on the ice. She shook her legs out and marked her jumps.

"Please welcome our next skater. Representing the Arctic Circle Figure Skating Club, Madison Albright."

Madison took her starting position yet again and took a deep breath before she started her program. She tried to listen to the music and to enjoy her performance. She focused on each move one at a time, even if it was only to lift an arm with grace and to the music. Madison prepped herself for the first jump and tried to avoid thinking too far ahead.

"Leg through," Madison said aloud as she took off. She held her breath and to her surprise and joy, she landed the jump perfectly. The crowd roared with applause. Obviously, most of the other girls had fallen on their double axels. Madison reminded herself to focus on what she needed to. She set up her triple toe. A brief thought of her fall at regionals crossed her mind, but she ignored it and replaced the thought with one of technique. She picked and vaulted into the air. Again she pulled out a smooth landing. Madison was into her performance now. She only had one jump left to go and then she would have nailed the program. Madison entered her spiral sequence and stretched her leg higher than ever. She executed her spin as fast as usual and set up for her last jump combination. Double Lutz-double loop. *Don't blow it,* she thought. *No, that's not what I'm supposed to think! What did Liz tell me? Oh yeah, reach, pull left shoulder back, right shoulder in.*

Madison did the footwork leading up to the jump and took off. The double Lutz landing was a little shaky but Madison managed the double loop. She let out a small whoop of joy, smiling, and started her last footwork sequence. She entered her final combination spin. She struck her final pose. The audience burst into applause.

Mrs. Albright was on her feet screaming and jumping. A few people were looking at her strangely but she didn't care. She caught Madison's eye as she bowed and winked at her. Madison skated to the edge of the ice and saw Liz beaming beside the boards. She pulled Madison into a huge hug.

"I am so proud of you. You did it. You even pulled the combination off," said Liz, her eyes shining.

Tears welled in Madison's eyes—happy tears. She passed the skaters waiting to skate and wished them good luck. By the time she entered the locker room her legs started to buckle. The performance had taken more out of her than she realized. She changed and went to look for her mom as her group finished up. She didn't want to watch anybody else until she was done with both her short and long.

"I'm so proud of you!" her mom exclaimed behind her. Madison wheeled around just in time to be swept up into her mother's arms. "I knew you could do it. Are you happy?" she asked.

"Yes," said Madison, craning her neck to see if new results had been posted.

Mrs. Albright frowned. "Your results are not what today is about, Madison," she said disapprovingly. "It's fine to want to place high, but your ranking should not make you feel any better or worse about how you skated."

"I know," Madison said with some annoyance. Of course it still meant a lot to her to place high. Her mom didn't seem to understand that. Madison saw a woman post a piece of paper on the wall behind her mother. Mrs. Albright turned around when she saw Madison's intense stare.

"Go check," she said reluctantly. 'But remember what I said."

Madison happily walked over to the results. She wasn't afraid to check her place today. She scanned the window for her group and then scanned the list for her name. She didn't have to look far. She was in second place! For a minute Madison felt a stab of disappointment that she wasn't first. Then she shook the thought out her mind. Second was still good, and just over two points separated her total score from that of the first-place skater for the short.

Madison tried to keep in mind that the fact that she was able to skate so well was a win in itself. It might be corny, but it was true. Madison felt good about the way she skated, and after she checked the results board, she realized that it really wouldn't have mattered if she placed first or last as long as she did her job on the ice. She raced back to her mom to tell her the good news but bumped into Liz first.

"Did you see? I'm in second," Madison said happily.

Liz broke out into a smile. "You did so well today! You can celebrate but keep your focus. You have to do the same thing for the long program tomorrow." Leave it to Liz to spoil the moment by getting all serious.

"I know, but can't I just be happy?" Madison asked, looking up at Liz.

"I guess that couldn't hurt. Go tell your mom. I still want you to come to practice tonight, though."

Madison agreed to be there and went to find her mom, who waited by the entrance.

"Second!" she shouted. Mrs. Albright gave her the thumbs up. Madison caught up with her and hugged her tightly.

"Let's go celebrate."

"I don't know the first place skater."

Mrs. Albright looked at Madison. "None of that. Don't think about her and what she can do. Focus on you."

Madison hung her head. "I guess I still have a lot to work on," she said sheepishly.

"Learning to be mentally tough takes time. But you're doing great. Let's go."

A happy Madison exited the ice rink ready to celebrate the day's accomplishments. Her confidence was growing by the minute. She had a few hours to revel in her great skate before she was back on the ice to practice for her long.

chapter

27

Pushing the Limits

"I don't understand!" Madison was fuming and pacing her hotel room floor.

"Calm down. It's normal to have a relapse," Mrs. Albright said.

"The day before the long? When I'm in second place? When I could win?" Madison's voice rose an octave with each sentence.

"Don't you see?" Mrs. Albright tried to get a word in. "Worrying about winning is why you had a bad practice today. You competed well because you focused only on what you needed to do at that moment. And now you're back to worrying about the result. It doesn't work to focus on the judging rather than the skating."

"I can't seem to stop thinking about it!" Madison wailed.

"That's not true. You managed to let that go for a few minutes during your short program today, and look what happened. You skated great. Can't you do that again?"

Madison bit her lip. She remembered how great it felt to skate well when she focused and relaxed.

"I just got a little ahead of myself at this afternoon's practice. I forgot to do all the exercises you showed me. I can pull myself together by tomorrow morning."

Mrs. Albright smiled and looked at the clock. "It's still early. Maybe you want to go out and explore Washington. Maybe get some dinner?"

"Okay," Madison agreed. Her mother's plan was to distract her from the competition and she had no problem with that.

Washington, D.C., was a bigger and busier town than Madison was used to. They went out around five o'clock. Although the weekend had begun, there were many workers from the shops and government offices hurrying home. They weren't smiling and passed each other without any acknowledgment.

Madison felt a sudden pride in the friendliness of her hometown. She and her mother walked the typical touristy landmarks—memorials, museums, and government buildings— and Madison wished that she could spend more time soaking up the attractions. They ate dinner at a small Italian restaurant and then headed back to the hotel. The little expedition had worked. Madison was feeling much better by the time she arrived in her hotel room. For a few hours, Madison had almost forgotten why she was in Washington, D.C.

"Thanks, mom. I feel so much better."

"I'm glad. On that note, get ready for bed. You have an early start time tomorrow."

"Why do they always do that to us?" Madison grumbled.

"All part of being a figure skater," Mrs. Albright noted. They laughed and Madison hurried to get ready for bed. She went to bed that night feeling pretty confident that tomorrow would be a good day.

28

chapter

Maddie Takes the Ice

Madison awoke before her alarm on Sunday morning. Her adrenaline was kicking in and she couldn't sleep any longer. Madison couldn't say that her focus was gone, but she was definitely more on edge and anxious today. It was five in the morning. She didn't have to get up for another hour and a half. Madison wished she could go out and compete right now— just get moving and go skate. She knew she would relax once she was warming up, but waiting was torture.

At six thirty Mrs. Albright's alarm went off. "Are you up?" she asked Madison.

"Have been for a while."

"Oh, no. Sweetie, I'm sorry."

"I'm fine. I just want to get a move on."

"You must be excited."

"Sort of."

"Well, start getting ready. We don't have that long before we have to leave."

To Madison's delight, time started to speed up as soon as they began to dress, apply make-up, and gather their bags. They arrived at the arena in record time despite Washington traffic and soon Madison got her wish: She was in the locker room getting ready to skate her long program.

Madison pulled her shiny pink dress out of the bag. She dressed and went about putting her hair up. Lifting her hair into a bun, she noticed that something had been added on the right sleeve of her costume—a tiny strip of fluttery red fabric. Madison smiled. Mom must have sewn it on to resemble the towel Liz whipped at her during training. Madison shook her head. She could hear her mom whispering, "If you ever get nervous, think back to what you do in practice." Now Madison would have a little reminder throughout her whole program. Madison took her place among the other girls at the gate and waited for her group to be announced.

"Will the finalists in Intermediate Ladies please take the ice?" the announcer boomed.

The competitors shot like a rocket through the doorway. This warm-up had a more intense vibe than Madison had ever experienced. Well, this was a national championship final! Any of these top five skaters could win. And everyone wanted to make sure that she got her shot at it. Out of the corner of her eye, Madison saw some near collisions. Everyone skated so fast coming from all angles! But every time Madison got nervous, she looked at the red strip flying under her eyes and thought back to her accomplishments over the past few weeks. That helped her push harder focus on the moment. The announcer called time and the competitors cleared the ice.

They skated in reverse order of their placement. That meant that Madison would be skating second to last. She had a long time to wait before she actually skated. Liz ushered her into an unused locker room so she could be alone.

Liz held her attention. "All right. You know what you have to do. Just what you did yesterday for your short: Take deep breaths and focus on one thing at a time."

Madison nodded as she rocked back and forth in time to the song she was listening to. She distanced herself from the outside world and focused on the one thing she needed to do. Liz kept checking to see what skater was on as Madison continued to do her breathing exercises and muscle tensing and relaxing. She could feel the tension ease away and she opened her eyes.

"I'm ready," she declared.

"Good. Because you're next," Liz said. They walked out of the locker room and Madison immediately put her earbuds in to block out the noise. She turned her back to the ice and visualized her performance. Soon Liz gave her a slight nod and Madison prepped to step onto the ice. This was it. Everything she had done up to this point was something to be proud of, but her true test was making it through this performance. Madison did knee bends at the boards while Liz gave last-minute advice. Liz clasped Madison's hands in hers. "You can do this," she reassured her. Madison bowed her head and nodded.

"Will you help me give our next skater a warm round of applause? Please welcome Madison Albright, representing the Arctic Circle Figure Skating Club."

Cheers filled the stadium as Madison skated to her starting position. The extra applause jarred her. She shakily took her starting pose. The Spanish guitar filled the arena and Madison began to glide. She opened with her layback spin. An awed gasp from the viewers meant she was off to a good start. Her double axel was first and Madison recalled the words Liz had said over and over. She jumped into the air and her landing had an extra glide that only much higher-level skaters mastered. Madison's heart soared and she was motivated to keep going strong.

The triple toe was the next jump. Madison showed no fear entering it. She leapt into the air from muscle memory and came down with as smooth a landing as her first jump had. *Yes!* Madison thought. The triple toe was her hardest jump. That done, she stepped into her circular footwork. Her feet moved with precision and grace as she plowed through the sequence and into her next two jumps, both of which were flawless.

Madison perked up even more halfway through the program. She was skating great and she didn't feel anxious at all. When the music sped up, so did she. She added authentic Spanish movements to her program. It was as if all her inhibitions were released—she skated from the heart. The audience could feel her emotion and they were right behind her, pushing her on to skate her best.

In what felt like mere seconds, Madison was taking off for her last combination jump. It was a double flip-double toe. If she landed it, she would get bonus points because it came so late in the program. Madison went up and landed the jump. Relief flooded over her and her feet started to fly even faster across the ice through the last few seconds of her program. Madison enjoyed each remaining second she was on the ice. This was why she skated: To feel the overwhelming satisfaction of skating that perfect program and skating it the best she could at that moment.

Madison pulled out of her last spin and finished with a flourish. The audience burst into rousing applause. Madison jumped up and down as soon as her music ended. She took her time taking her bows, picking up the flowers and teddy bears people tossed on the ice in congratulations, and enjoying all the attention. Finally, the applause died down and she skated over to Liz, who beamed with pride.

"Two great performances in a row! You did it! I'm so proud of you. Do you know how hard it was to overcome all you did?" She hugged her.

"I'm happy, too. I did it! It felt so good. I want to get out there and do it again."

"You will soon enough. Now you get to rest and let down. You did your job."

"I *am* kind of tired."

Madison and Liz sat in the Kiss and Cry area awaiting Madison' scores. In the new international judging system used at nationals, Madison would be able to hear her point total right away.

"And the composite score for Madison Albright is 108.06 points."

Madison breathed a sigh of relief. That score was definitely high enough to put her in first for now. But would it be enough to beat Jamie, who had placed first with her short program?

Liz advised, "Take your skates off and go find your mom."

But Madison stayed rinkside. She wanted to see the first-place skater's performance. Jamie passed her to begin her skate. She had beautiful extension and good speed. Madison watched apprehensively as Jamie landed her first jump. Madison couldn't help but wish Jamie would fall. Soon Jamie was almost through with her program, still skating without any mistakes. Then she took off smoothly for her second to last jump. When it was time to check out, Jamie just sat down on the ice. Madison sucked in a breath. Jamie had fallen! The deductions she'd get from her scores for that gave room for

Madison to win now. Madison's heart raced at that thought and she looked over at Liz, who obviously was thinking the same thing. The fall shook Jamie's confidence, and she missed her last jump as well. Two deductions! Now Madison definitely had a chance to win.

It was Jamie's turn to wait anxiously in the Kiss and Cry now. Jamie got off the ice and Madison saw her look of disappointment and the tears in her eyes. Madison's heart went out to her. She knew exactly how Jamie felt. After a few moments of tense silence, the announcer called out Jamie's component score of 37.81 for the short, then today's long: 68.52. Madison had a feeling that she might win but was too superstitious to think it in case she was wrong.

"Jamie's total score is 106.33," the announcer called. Madison waited, barely breathing, for the announcer to list the final ranking.

Then she let out a shriek. She had won! At 108.06, her total final score was almost two points higher than Jamie's! Madison raced to find Liz and her mother. She couldn't believe that she had gone from not even qualifying for Junior Nationals to winning the whole event.

The Zamboni came on the ice and just like that, Junior Nationals was over—all except the awards ceremony, that is.

"Congratulations, Madison," called several skaters as Madison rushed by them.

"Mom! Mom!" Madison screamed when she saw Mrs. Albright. "I won! I'm first!"

Mrs. Albright's eyes widened. "That's tremendous! I know how much you wanted this. Did you tell Liz?"

"No" said Madison breathlessly. "I haven't seen her yet. Where is she?" Madison looked around.

"Looking for me, champion?" Liz said from behind her, wrapping Madison in a huge hug. "Congratulations! You deserve it!"

"It feels so great!"

"Well, come on. You have to go collect your medal center ice and take a picture on the podium. You have responsibilities now that you're the champ" Liz's eyes were shining.

Madison blushed and smiled. Mrs. Albright and Liz followed Madison and watched her climb atop the podium. She curtseyed to lower her head as officials placed the gold medal around it. The five finalists, Jamie in third, posed for photos, holding huge bouquets of flowers and smiling during the camera flashes.

The hours after learning she'd won swirled past like a whirlwind. Madison walked around in a daze; it was surreal. Madison didn't want to take any of it for granted. She tried to live in the moment and enjoy the spotlight.

Finally, she'd changed back to jeans and sweater, and her mother smiled to her and Liz, "Let's go celebrate."

"I think we have more than one thing to celebrate today," Liz said.

"Besides skating my best and winning?" Madison asked.

"Yes," Liz answered. "Do you have a passport?"

"I do," Madison said, puzzled. "Why?"

"U.S. Figure Skating sends its Junior Champions overseas to represent America at international competitions. So I hope you're ready to pack your bags, because you're going to Europe early next year."

"What?" Madison's mouth dropped open. "Awesome. I've never been there! I can't wait to go." Mrs. Albright still looked a bit shocked, but Madison was ready for anything.

"What will we do with the puppy while we're away?" Mrs. Albright smiled at Madison.

"A puppy? Really?" Madison's eyes shined.

"You held up your end of the bargain. Now we'll hold up ours." Mrs. Albright promised, "But you are not getting the dog because you won. You are getting her because you were able to overcome your fears."

"Right, mom," Madison said. "Thank you, thank you, thank you!" She held her mother tightly. "This is the best day."

"There's plenty of it left. Let's go get something to eat," Mrs. Albright said. "You have to call your dad when we get to the restaurant."

Madison, her mom, and her coach linked arms and walked out of the rink. Medal still swinging from her neck, Madison phoned her father and told him the news. He was thrilled for her and couldn't wait to hear about her trip. And Madison couldn't wait to tell him.

"I'll tell you all about it on the way to pick out my dog," Madison giggled.

There was so much to look forward to. Madison couldn't wait to get home and get started on next season. Who knew? The next time she competed, she could be skating in Europe. And Madison could not wait for the challenge.

A Message from Nicolette House

Like Madison, I have loved figure skating since I was very young. I learned to skate about the same time I learned to walk. My parents are deeply involved in the sport. If I am away from skating for even a short time, I feel like something is missing in my life and get right back to it.

I have been blessed with great parents, athletic ability, great coaches, and opportunities to pursue my skating dreams. I hope you have a passion for healthy pursuits like skating that are challenging—both physically and mentally—that help give you direction and bring you energy and enthusiasm. I hope you will act on your dreams like Maddie.

Sports and performance are great ways to express yourself, have fun, and build confidence. But disappointments are bound to come along. You just have to stay positive about yourself and your abilities and you'll work through them. As long as you continue to pursue your dreams, you've already won! That's true whether you are mastering a difficult tune on the piano or working to land your double axel. All those hours of work and dedication will pay off as long as you keep trying.

Being involved in a sport will teach you things that you can use your whole life. Teamwork, dedication, and passion are all essential tools in sports and in life. I'm a college student and a professional skater now. I can juggle both because of the skills I've learned through dedication to my sport.

Thank you for reading my book. I hope you will write me a letter (at the Sporting Chance Press address on this book) and tell me about yourself and how you liked the story. I look forward to hearing from you.

— Nicolette House

Figure Skating Elements

Figure skating performances involve *jumps, spins,* and *footwork.* These are the *elements* that the judges watch closely and grade when you compete. Elements are the athletic actions required or chosen in a skating competition depending upon the level and the stage of the event.

■ Jumps

Did you ever try to jump and spin in the air at the same time? Maybe you do jumps in ballet or gymnastics. Jumps are one of the fundamental elements of figure skating. In a jump, the skater leaps into the air, rotates one or more revolutions, and lands. Jumps are identified or named by how the skater takes off and lands, and by the number of rotations completed.

There are two essential types of figure skating jumps: *edge jumps* and *toe jumps.* Edge jumps start on the edge or the long portion of the skate blade. Toe jumps start on the toe pick—the special serrated (saw-toothed) front of the figure skate blade.

Skaters move in different ways to prepare for these elements. They might lean way over in one direction, then move in another, shifting their weight as they perform the element. When you watch skating, notice the moves skaters make before they jump. How they prepare for the jump has a big impact on whether they perform the jump well.

Jumps are made from both the inside and outside edges of the skate's blade. Are you wondering which is the inside and which is the outside? Imagine you are wearing skates, standing with your legs spread apart and you drop a water balloon straight down between your feet—*splash.* It would be the inside edges of your skate blades that get most wet.

A skater might use the right or the left foot to start the jump; the skater may go forward or backward; and the skater may start on the inside or outside edge.

In most competitions, six jumps are considered jump elements. Edge jumps include the loop, the axel and the salchow; toe jumps include the toe loop, the flip, and the Lutz. If you watch skating on TV, you hear these terms all the time.

If you all ready skate, you probably know them, but this list may help you explain them to your friends.

Edge Jumps

LOOP–The skater takes off on a back outside edge and lands on the same back outside edge to perform a loop.

AXEL—A difficult jump that precedes double jumps, the axel is the only jump in which the skater takes off from the forward position. The skater takes off from the outside edge of one foot and lands on the back outside edge of the opposite foot to perform an Axel. A single Axel consists of 1.5 revolutions, a double is 2.5 revolutions, and a triple is 3.5 revolutions. The extra half revolution or .5 tells you that the skater faces forward at the start of the jump, but ends up facing backward at the end. It is named after its inventor, Norwegian figure skater, Axel Paulsen.

SALCHOW (sal•kou)—The skater takes off from the back inside edge of one foot and lands on the back outside edge of the opposite foot to perform the Salchow. This jump was created by Swedish figure skater, Ulrich Salchow.

Toe Jumps

TOE LOOP—The skater performs a toe loop by using a toe pick to assist a jump that takes off and lands on the same back outside edge.

FLIP—The skater performs a flip jump using a toe-pick to assist a jump that takes off from the back inside edge of one foot and lands on the back outside edge of the opposite foot.

LUTZ (luhts)—The skater completes a Lutz using a toe-pick to assist a jump that takes off from a back outside edge of one foot and lands on the back outside edge of the opposite foot. The Lutz was created by Austrian figure skater, Alois Lutz.

■ Spins

Did you ever wonder how it would feel to spin super fast like a top? Spins are a lot of fun and require athleticism. Spins are fundamental to figure skating and are another required element in figure skating competition. The skater performs a spin by holding one or more body positions while rotating, centered on a single point on the ice. In other words, when you spin, you keep your head, arms and legs fairly still until you change your spin position or end it. There are many varieties of spins.

Each type of spin has its own beginning movements, but the spin itself begins with the *hook*—you are moving in one direction and you change from forward motion to circular motion. Once you begin that motion, you are pulling yourself towards an axis or specific point on the ice. You begin a rotation on the blade just behind the toe pick where your weight is placed on the ball of the foot. This spin motion from a single point on the ice creates centripetal force—a force that pushes you inward. When you pull your extremities (arms, legs, head) in, the speed of the spin increases. When you extend your extremities outward, the spin slows and comes to an end. A skater is a master at using physics and the laws of motion. A skater needs good centering, balance, and conservation of energy to perform spins well.

The three basic spin positions are the ***upright, sit, and camel***.

UPRIGHT SPIN—In the upright spin, the skater rotates with an extended skating leg, which is not a camel position. Upright spins include the *scratch* spin, the *layback* spin, and the *Biellmann* spin.

SIT SPIN—In the sit spin, the skater rotates in a sitting position with the body low to the ice, bending the knee on the leg that carries the skater's weight while the free leg is extended beside it. Sit spins includes the *sit spin*, the *pancake spin* and the *cannon ball*.

CAMEL SPIN—In the camel spin, the skater spins on one leg while the free leg is extended in the air in a higher position than the hip and parallel to the ice. Camel spins include the camel spin and the doughnut spin.

■ Footwork

Footwork is the third fundamental element in figure skating competition. In *Maddie Takes the Ice*, Caitlin tells Maddie that her footwork is not good. She says that the judges won't be able to tell what she's trying to do.

Skaters must move around the ice with precision, agility and grace. Footwork is what gets you from one skating element to the next. Footwork is also a sequence of steps that takes the skater across the ice in straight, circular, or winding patterns. Competition often requires a particular step sequence that combines turns, hops and edge changes. The designs these movements make used to be the most important element of skating competition, in fact, these "figures" or marks gave the sport its name—figure skating. Have you heard of a figure 8? Some skaters can make a perfect figure 8 on the ice!

Endless Possibilities

Whether you watch skating performances or skate yourself, there are many opportunities for athleticism and art in the sport even in the most basic movements. When a skater is just moving across the ice, the skater may perform a *spiral*, a move in which a skater demonstrates grace and flexibility by extending the nonskating leg behind into the air during a long glide. As the skater approaches a curve or a circle and needs to gain speed and power quickly for the next element, the skater uses a challenging stroking technique called *crossovers*, in which the skater crosses one foot over the other to accelerate. Like all great sports, skating offers endless possibilities of expression.

Questions about *Maddie Takes the Ice*

1. What makes Madison an interesting character?

2. What bothers Madison at regionals?

3. How did Madison's troubles impact her performance at regionals?

4. How was Madison's life different from Jordan's?

5. Is Caitlin a bully? What advice would you have given Madison about handling Caitlin?

6. How would you react to Jillian's suggestions about eating if you were Madison?

7. What are the most important conflicts in the story?

8. At the end of the story, what has Madison learned about how to handle problems?

9. Was Madison's "date" with Peter a good idea?

10. When things bother you, do you talk to your parents and others who can help?